# Militant Christianity

## An urgent heart cry for radical Kingdom advancement

## Jonathan Conrathe

Sovereign World

Sovereign World Ltd
PO Box 777
Tonbridge
Kent TN11 0ZS
England

*Email*: info@sovereign-world.com
*Website* www.sovereign-world.com

ISBN 1 85240 353 5

Typeset be CRB Associates, Reepham Norfolk
Cover design by CCD, www.ccdgroup.co.uk
Printed by Clays, St Ives plc

# Dedication and Appreciation

When one looks back over the years and considers how many wonderful people God has used to shape your life and ministry, to be a support and a friend, an encourager and confidante, it seems almost impossible to name everyone. If it had to be *one* person, who else could it be but *Jesus*! After all, everything good in life comes from Him and often I have felt His love, support and encouragement through friends, family and ministry associates. Often His wisdom for difficult situations, His correction when I needed to hear it, His generous provision through the willing hearts of His saints. So first and foremost, I dedicate this book to My wonderful Lord and Saviour, Jesus Christ, for Whom and by Whom I live and minister, and without Whom I am nothing. It is my sincere prayer that He will use this publication to stir, provoke, encourage, motivate and build up His Body and thrust forth many labourers for the Gospel to the ends of the earth and usher in the Kingdom of God in our generation.

All that said, I could not let this book go out without expressing my heartfelt gratitude to my wife, Elaine (always there for me, loving, standing with me and believing in me – you are a gift beyond words! Thanks for sacrificing all that precious family time so that I could write.); my parents (mum and dad, you have been such an example and encouragement of love, faith, giving and sacrifice – what can I say?). How can I express all the gratitude that I feel towards my brothers and sisters, my grandparents, and friends like David and Suzanne Prytherch who generously donated the laptop on which this book was written;

David and Sheena Pailthorpe who have stuck with me through thick and thin; Alastair and Heather Whitmoor-Pryer, Robert Stockwell and my trustees – at times like these one realises what a wonderful network of friends and support God has given us – thank you to you all! I am also indebted to Don and Heather Double for the years of training and encouragement you put into me – surely you gave me some of the finest training in the world, may the Lord bless you and make you ever fruitful in Him. There are so many others that I would like to thank, such as Charles and Joyce Sibthorpe, Derek and Irene Brown, Steve Thomas and Barney Coombes, Theresia Wairimu, Bob and Hilda Gordon (Bob now with Jesus), David Ndarahutse (a true apostle – now also with Jesus), the leadership of Cheam C.C., David Pawson, Derek Prince, T.L. Osborn, Kenneth Copeland, Reinhard Bonnke – some of you I have met and some not, but I am deeply grateful to God for your inspiring and godly example, and your teaching and faith. The list could go on and on, but I must stop there for the sake of space! Thank God for the wonderful and priceless gift of family, friends, mentors and partners – how we need one another!

I close as I began – to Jesus belongs all the praise, honour and glory, and to Him I dedicate this book, *Militant Christianity*, as a tool for the building up and equipping of His Church and the furtherance of the Gospel until He comes!

*Jonathan Conrathe*
February 2003
Surrey, England

# Contents

# *Introduction*

## The Way Things Are

The contents of this book are intended to be as provocative as its title. Provocative, *not* offensive. As the subtitle suggests, it is a cry from the heart. Dare I say, a cry from the heart of God. The state of our Western society, particularly here in the UK, demands a response from the Church that is somewhat more radical than what it is getting. A response that does not seek to be at peace with Western culture, but is truly *cross*-cultural! Having come through the so-called 'decade of evangelism' (which became almost the decade of 'non-evangelism' with statistics showing less evangelistic activity and church growth in the Western world than in the eighties!), the Church faces huge challenges as we seek to win our world for Christ in the twenty-first century. If the woes of the Chinese and Middle-Eastern Church can be summed up in the words 'persecution' and 'tribulation', the woes of the Western Church can certainly be summed up in 'cultural appeasement', 'humanism', 'unbelief' and 'maintenance-oriented passivity', at least by comparison with our African, South American and Asian brothers and sisters. England, which was once *the* missionary sending nation of the world, now has missionaries from Africa, South America and Asia coming back to us to 'pay a debt' which they feel they owe the Church in this nation because our forefathers lived and died for the gospel that changed their lives and nations for Christ. In the process, they bring with them a painful reminder of the prayerful commitment, raw faith and passionate sacrifice that left our shores with their own coffins already made, determined to bring the unsaved (note: not 'unchurched' – it's quite possible to be totally 'churched' and completely 'unsaved!'), to the foot of the cross. The aim of this book is threefold: to establish firmly the twenty-first-century believer in the eternal truths of God's Word that motivate great soul winners in the ministry of the Kingdom; to address some of the hindrances we face in the Western Church in fulfilling the Great Commission; and to provoke the reader to a new level of faith, consistency of walk with God, and a no compromise, *spiritually* aggressive approach to the salvation of our nation(s).

It is my sincere prayer to God that if there be any offence caused by this book, it will be only the offence of the cross, that instrument through which we are crucified to the world and the world is crucified to us (Galatians 6:14). The message of the cross is still the power of God (1 Corinthians 1:18), which God delights to confirm with signs following (Mark 16:20).

During the recent crisis in Afghanistan, I found myself reading an article in one of the national tabloids, comparing Islam with Christianity. The writer, not by any means claiming to be a believer, concluded by asking some penetrating questions about the Church's confidence in the gospel she preaches, wondering why there were no Christians boldly proclaiming on our streets that there is 'One God, and His Son, Jesus Christ!' I couldn't help but be deeply moved and saddened at the same time. Satan has always stepped into the void created by the Church's passivity. Today, while the Church seems convinced of her need to become 'culturally relevant' and 'seeker-friendly', Islam makes no apology and the occultists seduce the minds of our children. It is high time for a new (or, rather, once lost, now revived) breed of Christianity to arise and take the Kingdom by force! (That is the force of proclamation and demonstration of the Kingdom of God, *not* physical or military force!)

God is looking for a place of agreement in the Western world, that will believe that He is the same covenant-keeping, miracle-working God in Europe as He is anywhere else! Faith is a choice and, at this critical time in history, the nature of our choices will determine the nature of our destiny. Generations to come lie in the balance!

There have been a number of significant experiences and ensuing convictions that have led to the writing of this book. I have personally been privileged to preach the gospel in about twenty-seven different nations in the last fourteen years, as well as around the UK. My experiences in evangelism and church planting, coupled with a number of significant conversations with apostolic leaders and evangelists both in this country and overseas, lead me to raise some serious questions concerning the things that influence both our convictions and practice as far as evangelism and apostolic ministry is concerned in the Western world.

This book is my humble, though passionately heartfelt attempt to provoke an evangelistic revolution, to urge apostolic leaders to release their evangelists and not 'pastor-ise' them, to encourage a proactive approach to evangelism, rather than a mere passive expectation that one day revival will come and everything will be all right! So much talk of revival without some positive, faith-filled action will surely only lead the Body of Christ into a state where *'hope deferred makes the heart sick'* (Proverbs 13:12). Revival is God's business, evangelism is ours! I believe we are on the edge of the greatest move of God ever experienced by mankind, but until we are walking in the fullness of it, let's press on to reap the harvest God has given us! If not, we are in serious danger of allowing our convictions concerning a coming revival to lead us into a state of passivity, thus hindering all honest attempts at effective New Testament evangelism.

> 'It is a shameful son who sleeps during harvest,
> but he who wins souls is wise!'          (see Proverbs 10:5)

At the end of 2001, it was recorded that the late George Harrison (member of The Beatles) had lived for many years with the following three fundamental questions in his heart: 'Why am I here?', 'What am I here for?' and 'Where am I going?' Without drawing any conclusions on George Harrison's eternal destiny, we can all identify with his three poignant questions. There are obvious theological answers to all three, but it is the third question that confronts us most powerfully with the stark reality of that awesome privilege and responsibility God has given us all. The power of *choice*. This life is, in reality, the only opportunity we will ever have to make any eternal difference to another human being's existence. While building bridges with our communities, being seeker-friendly, carrying out acts of mercy, etc., all have their place in Kingdom ministry, helping us to make connection with the unsaved, it is the gospel, and the gospel alone that ultimately changes lives (Romans 1:16). In the midst of all the teaching concerning the *process* of coming to faith in Christ, let us never forget that it is the *crisis* point of conversion that takes someone out of the domain of Satan into the wonderful Kingdom of God through the power of new creation. It is the job of the evangelist to bring people to that point of crisis in the power of the Holy Spirit and to equip the Church to do the same (Ephesians 4:12).

May God so use this small publication to release evangelists from the fear of confrontation to fulfil their divine mandate and to urge apostles to broaden their horizons in God beyond the realm of government and administration into the signs of an apostle, proclaiming the gospel in the power and demonstration of the Holy Spirit. And, lastly, may it become a great encouragement, building faith and expectation in the great mass of believers in our churches throughout the Western world so brimming with potential and longing to be used of God. May an unflinching conviction fill your heart that God moves not with the man or woman who is necessarily perfect and mature, but rather with those who are simply prepared to step out by faith and expect great things from a great God!

# Chapter 1

## Evangelism – Why?
## (Our Conviction and Message)

### Eleven reasons why we should be winning the lost

In this first chapter my aim is simple. To help create the convictions that motivate evangelism. Discussion of strategies and methods at this stage, without the presence of firm biblical convictions, would be like trying to start an engine without any fuel, or lighting a fire without the raw materials necessary to do so. Although we so desperately need to be full of the Holy Spirit in our evangelism, we cannot afford to be low in our intake of the Word of God which so powerfully strengthens our inner man, imparts faith to our spirit, and creates the conviction of eternal realities that motivates the heart to action in the gospel. Join me as we start to lay the biblical foundations that establish us in a life committed to winning souls for the Kingdom of God.

### 1. He has changed our lives

The heat, or rather the humidity, was unbearable, the air dusty, the journey long, and the road typically bumpy for a developing nation. We were in Mindanoa, the Muslim-dominated part of the Philippine islands, notoriously dangerous for local pastors and travelling missionaries alike. I was sharing an open-backed truck with about thirteen other men, all native Filipinos, and all with a criminal record of one description or another. Following an hour or so of joyful praise as we bumped along the dusty track on our way to do another mission, the brothers began to share their testimonies one by one. Coming from the safe, leafy suburbs of Surrey, England, as each man shared his story, my emotions went through something akin to a rollercoaster experience, from slight anxiety, to shock, raw amazement, and finally sheer wonder at the transforming power of the grace of God! Each one of these new believers had at one time or another killed in cold blood, whether through involvement with extreme political factions, terrorists or as an expression of sheer anger in the midst of relational conflict. Yet here we were together, singing, praying and sharing testimonies of God's miraculous grace and power, with smiles on our faces and joy in our hearts. These men had no question at all as to why they were in the business of sharing the Good News about Jesus with others. It was simple. He had changed their lives.

We may not all have such a radical testimony as these men (radical in its extremes), but as believers we are all 'living letters of Christ' (2 Corinthians 3:3), and our testimonies are powerful tools in the hands of God to win others to Jesus. The simple truth is that not everyone relates to having once been a multiple murderer, now an evangelist. But some do! Whatever our life experience, whatever our testimony, there is someone out there just like you, who needs to hear what God has done for you. Every testimony is vital and valid for the cause of the gospel.

In John 4 we have the well-known account of Jesus talking to a Samaritan woman who had come to draw water from the well where He had sat down to rest. In this prophetic divine appointment, Jesus brings the woman to a place of spiritual thirst for the living waters of eternal life. Following her expressed desire for such 'living waters', Jesus tenderly exposes, by a word of knowledge, the very thing that stands in the way of her receiving eternal life: her immorality.

In verses 28–30 we see the powerful effect of this woman's testimony as she goes back into the town telling the people (who quite possibly knew her lifestyle),

> *'Come, see a Man who told all things that I ever did. Could this be the Christ?'*     (John 4:29)

The people followed her back to meet with Jesus. Although verses 39–42 clearly proclaim that many more believed in Christ when they heard Him for themselves, it was the woman who brought them to Him, and verse 39 plainly declares that many of the Samaritans believed in Him, *'because of the word of the woman'*! Every one of us has a testimony that shines like a bright light in a darkened room. What God has done for us, He will do for anyone who believes on Him: He has changed our lives not only for our benefit, but also for the benefit of every life we will ever touch (2 Corinthians 1:3–4). You are the light of the world (Matthew 5:14). Let it shine!

## 2. We are compelled by love

Arguably the best-known verse in the Bible, John 3:16 clearly states it was the unlimited, unconditional (*agape*) love of God that motivated the Father to send Jesus to die as our substitute on the cross, paying the price for sins He neither committed nor was responsible for – the sins of the entire human race, past, present and future. In John 20:21 Jesus states that in just the same way as the Father sent Him, we are sent by Christ. We are ambassadors for Him, sent by that same unconditional love that brought salvation into this world in the first place!

The real burning question for many sincere hearts is, 'How can I really know that kind of love for those who don't know Christ?' The reality is that while we can and do know God's love in our hearts by the Spirit of God within us (Romans 5:5; Galatians 5:22), the Apostle Paul makes it clear in 2 Corinthians 5:14–21 that it is the truth of what God has done for us in Christ, through the cross, that produces such compelling love for the lost. The word 'compel' in New Testament Greek is *sunecho*, essentially meaning 'to hold together' or 'grip tightly'. It is used in a variety of different settings but in every use of the word there is a sense of constraint, a tight grip that prevents escape (*Strong's Exhaustive Concordance of the Bible*). Quite a thought when you consider how the Master in Jesus' wedding feast parable commands his servants to go into the highways and *compel* them to come in! This truly is a 'compelling' love!

Paul explains what he means in this way:

- Since Christ died for all people, then all people died in Him. Sin is thus paid for and all those who receive Him are free to live a new life as new creations in Christ.

- God *has* reconciled us to Himself through Christ.

- God *has* given us a responsibility, a ministry, and committed *to us* the word of reconciliation, i.e. to tell others that God has removed their sins in Christ, and declares righteous (right in His sight) anyone who believes that God raised Jesus from the dead and proclaims Him as Lord (Romans 10:9–10).

- We are now Christ's ambassadors in a fallen world.

Through my years of ministry in various different nations, God has given me the opportunity to minister personally to a few government leaders. It was on one such occasion, in Argentina, that I had the opportunity to lead a regional leader to a personal faith in Christ.

Before going to South America, I had made the commitment to the Lord that were He ever to open the corridors of power to me, then I would never leave the office of a government leader without first challenging him or her as to where they stood with Christ. That prayer turned out to be prophetic, indeed, as I had the privilege of leading three government leaders to Christ on that one trip alone.

On the first night of our mission to Los Antiguos, a young teenage girl came forward for prayer for her back condition, and was instantly healed, leading also to her surrendering her life to the Lord. In the midst of her joy, she asked me if I would please visit her father who was suffering with bouts of repeated depression. I asked her who her father was, and she told me he was the governor of that region and would send a car to bring me to their government offices the next day, if I was willing to come. I responded positively and the next day was escorted to her father's office. Once we had got past the usual formalities, the Governor asked me what I thought would be the greatest thing he could do for the people he served. I promptly replied, 'You should give them a "born-again" governor!' Sensing his reaction (a mixture of shock and conviction), I chose to take the lower ground (or higher ground as the case may be!), and said, 'But before we do anything about that, I first need to ask your forgiveness, sir.' Looking surprised, the Governor responded, 'Whatever for?' I replied, 'I am not here to discuss the rights and wrongs of the Falklands War, but one thing is certain: the loss of wives' husbands and children's fathers is regrettable in any situation. I stand here representing a higher government than either the Argentinian or British governments, I am an ambassador for Jesus Christ. Now, representing the British people, since I am an Englishman also, I beg your forgiveness for what we have done to your people.' The Governor looked at me silently, with tears in his eyes, and gave his forgiveness. I urged him to receive Jesus as His Lord and Saviour, understanding that it was He who had given him this place of office and to Him the Governor would give account. Bowing his head, with tears, he surrendered his life to Christ. Following on from the Governor's conversion, and increased prayer warfare on behalf of the local church leaders and ourselves, God moved in a powerful way bringing many in that town to salvation as the Lord confirmed His Word with signs and wonders. We are ambassadors for Christ. We do not live under the government of this world system but under the government and resources of the Kingdom of heaven! Let's remember who we are in Him, whom we represent. For it is in His authority (which is *all* authority in heaven and on earth, Matthew 28:18–19) that we go, in His anointing and sufficiency that we minister (2 Corinthians 1:21; 3:5), and in His grace that we stand (Romans 5:2).

### 3. We are responsible before God for our generation

As we move into our next couple of points, I must warn you in advance that they are very 'weighty' or 'heavy' points. One of the marks of current Western culture is that it has become very 'self-oriented', leading to a distinct dislike of terms such as 'responsibility', 'accountability', 'discipline' or, worse still, 'duty'! We prefer to 'feel' like doing something, to be 'inspired' rather than 'responsible' (although I believe we can be responsible *and* inspired!). However, Jesus is looking for those who don't just feel good because they've led someone to Christ, finding a personal sense of reward in helping others, but rather He is looking for 'labourers' in the gospel. Interestingly, it is this quality of worker to which Jesus was referring when He said there are few and which He exhorted us to pray for the Lord of the harvest to 'thrust forth' (Matthew 9:37–38). We need more than short-term inspiration: we need long-term convictions which lead to true commitment in the work of the gospel.

Proverbs 24:11–12 states,

> *'Deliver those who are drawn toward death,*
> *And hold back those stumbling to the slaughter.*
> *If you say, "Surely we did not know this,"'*
> *Does not He who weighs the hearts consider it?*
> *He who keeps your soul, does He not know it?*
> *And will He not render to each man according to his deeds?'*

As an evangelist, I am often asked, 'But what about those who have never heard the gospel? Where will they go (in terms of eternity)?' Although Scripture does give us answers to such questions (Romans 2:12–16, for example), I normally end up reminding enquirers of (1) their responsibility, since they *do know* the gospel, and (2) the responsibility of the Church to share the Good News of Jesus with those who have not yet heard.

In the months immediately preceding the great Welsh Revival, young Evan Roberts (whom God used as His main human instrument in that move of His Spirit) felt compelled to pray all night for his nation. During the early hours of the morning, God gave him an open vision (a vision he could see in front of him, as if watching a movie) of thousands of people walking towards the edge of a great cliff, totally oblivious of the terrible fall immediately in front of them into what seemed like eternal hell fire at the bottom of the cliff. Deeply moved in his spirit, Evan Roberts cried out to God to let him stand at the edge of that great cliff face for two years, to hold the people back and save them from such an awful end. Remarkably, the Welsh revival lasted just two years, in which some 200,000 people were swept into the Kingdom of God. Oh that we would take hold of our responsibility in God! No one can do everything, but everyone can do something! Did that discouraged itinerant tent evangelist know what he was doing when he led a young Billy Graham to Christ, in the face of virtually no other conversions through a long tent campaign? And what about that dear Methodist circuit preacher who preached to a near empty chapel, not knowing that a young Charles Spurgeon was standing outside, listening intently at the door, surrendering his life to Christ? If we will only be obedient, just as David served his generation by the will of God (Acts 13:36), we will see that our God does mighty things with small acts of obedience. It is the 'seed-principle' of the Kingdom of God (Mark 4:26–32).

In closing this point, we would do well to consider the Lord's admonition to Ezekiel in Ezekiel 3:17–21. We do not want 'blood' on our hands when we stand before the King. We may well say that this was a specific word to Ezekiel, as an Old Testament prophet – granted! However, when we look over to the New Testament, we must also consider Jesus' parables of the wise and foolish virgins (with its message to stay full of the oil of the Holy Spirit that flows from a life-giving, intimate relationship with Jesus), the talents (gifts are given with responsibility: God wants us to use them, and will reward or judge us according to what we have done with the stewardship He has given us), and the sheep and the goats (the only difference in Jesus' eyes is what people do or don't do in terms of acts of mercy and compassion). Before we move on to more 'exciting, feel-good' points, I have one more 'weighty' point to make. Stay with me, it's all fundamental to our convictions and motivation in the gospel.

### 4. The prospect of eternal judgement – heaven or hell?

Oswald J. Smith said, 'No one has the right to hear the gospel twice, until everyone has heard it once!' Why such urgency, such passionate communication? The Scriptures urge us,

> 'Seek the LORD **while He may be found;**
> Call upon Him **while He is near.**
> Let the wicked forsake his way,
> And the unrighteous man his thoughts;
> Let him return to the LORD,
> And He will have mercy on him;

*And to our God,*
*For He will abundantly pardon.'*                          (Isaiah 55:6–7)[1]

There is an urgency that comes through the whole of Scripture with regard to our response to the Word of God.

*'Behold **now** is the accepted time, behold **now** is the day of salvation.'*                          (2 Corinthians 6:2)

*'**Today**, if you will hear His voice,*
***Do not harden your hearts.'***                          (Hebrews 4:7)

There are primarily two words in New Testament Greek trans-lated in our Bibles as 'time'. One is *chronos* (a length or season of time), the other is *kairos* (a moment in time, appointed time). It is the latter that is used to describe the moment of response to the gospel. It is urgent! It is all very well having an 'Engel scale' (a scale developed by James F. Engel to help us understand at what point somebody is in the process of coming to Christ), but quite frankly, although such scales and statistics may be interesting, even helpful, we are not called by God to assess where someone is at before we preach the gospel to him or her! He alone knows where each individual heart stands before Him. We may well develop a sensitivity to the Holy Spirit in discerning the state of an individual's heart, but none the less it is vital that we never lose sight of the eternal stakes! Without Christ, humanity is hopelessly lost, headed for a godless eternity in unceasing torment (Romans 3:23; Ephesians 2:12; Matthew 25:41). I remember leading a man in his mid-fifties to Christ on a Sunday morning in Cornwall, England. The man had just walked into the church and sat down. He had little, if any, experience or knowledge of Christianity, but just came in to see what was going on. I was not the speaker that morning, but somehow ended up in conversation with him over a cup of coffee at the end of the meeting. As I shared the gospel with him, the Lord really moved in his heart and he ended up praying with me to receive Jesus as His Lord and Saviour. The next day, as I drove through

---

[1] Unless otherwise stated, the emphasis made in scriptural quotations is mine.

the town, I noticed a commotion by the roadside as paramedics were trying to resuscitate a man who had just collapsed. I later discovered it was the very man I had led to Christ the day before. He went to be with his Saviour that afternoon.

While we all greatly rejoice in the tremendous success of the Alpha course in the UK and around the world, and appreciate the process concept behind such courses, we can never afford to lose that vital sense of urgency when confronting people with their need of Christ. If that man had not been led to Christ on the Sunday morning, he may well have been in hell by the following afternoon. In recent years I have become increasingly disturbed by the failure of evangelists, trained in the 'seeker-friendly' mould, to confront people with their need of salvation. I have heard some fabulous presentations of the gospel, with discernible anointing on them, only to be disappointed at the failure to give an 'up-front' appeal for salvation. It has become popular to invite people who 'might want to know more' to stay behind for a 'chat' and perhaps introduce them to Alpha or give them a book. While it is great to invite people to Alpha, to be warm and approachable, to give free literature concerning the gospel, we must be aware that for some that message may have been God's last chance for them to escape hell and make it to heaven. D.L. Moody, the great nineteenth-century evangelist, described how he was preaching in a large wooden building in Chicago to an audience of 5,000 people, all crammed in to hear this famous minister. As he came to the end of his message, he uncharacteristically decided *not* to end his message that night with an appeal for salvation, but simply to close in prayer and release the people to go home, anticipating that he would have another chance the following night. However, as he finished his last words of prayer, a cry went up from the back of the hall, 'Fire! Fire! The building's on fire! Save yourselves!' Tragically, there were too many people in the building, and many were crushed to death in the ensuing panic. Moody, along with other ministers on the platform, managed to escape by a side entrance, but as he stood from a distance watching the flames engulf the building and hearing the desperate cries of people inside, he vowed to God, with tears in his eyes, that he would never preach again without giving people the opportunity to respond to the gospel. Brothers and sisters, fellow evangelists, church leaders, we have a salvation that is *'now'*, a God who is *'now'* (The I AM), and an eternity to face that is only a breath away. May God restore to us all an awareness of eternity, an urgency of spirit, and a genuine concern for those lost without Christ.

### 5. There is only one *Saviour and* one *Name by which we can be saved!*

Jesus said,

> *'I am the way, the truth and the life. No one comes to the Father except through Me.'*          (John 14:6)

The apostle Peter declared,

> *'Nor is there salvation in any other, for there is no other name under heaven given among men by which we must be saved.'*
>                                                           (Acts 4:12)

There is *no* other name, *no* other authority, personality, philosophy or system that can affect the salvation of the human soul. In today's pluralistic society, it is so vital that we truly believe and proclaim this most fundamental of truths. We do *not* serve the same God as other religions! As I travel around in the Western world, teaching and preaching, I often find myself urging the young people in today's churches to stop talking merely about 'God', and start talking about 'Jesus'. We live in a pluralistic society that feels no impact at all when Christians talk only about God, without making reference to Jesus. What 'God' are you talking about?! Satan laughs and mocks the Church when believers buy the demonic lie of 'multi-faith', and believe me, it is preparing the way for the Anti-Christ's one-world system with its one-world religion. In his letter John clearly states, *'Whoever denies the Son does not have the Father either'* (1 John 2:23). In 1 Corinthians 10:19–20, Paul addresses the issue of idols and concludes that what is offered to idols is offered to demons. An idol is anything that takes the place of God as He is revealed in Christ. What stands behind the religion of the Anti-Christ is the demonic. Satan masquerades himself in many forms, with many masks, and he is a religious counterfeiter. Nevertheless, despite the fact that there are many religions in this world, there are only two spiritual kingdoms, the Kingdom of God and the domain of Satan. The *only* way out of Satan's domain is to come in simple repentance and faith to the Lord Jesus Christ.

> 'For "**whoever** calls on the name of the LORD shall be saved!"'
> (Romans 10:13)

Many times, as I have stood on platforms around the world with fellow Christian leaders and together we have simply declared 'Jesus is Lord!', people have fallen on the floor writhing like snakes or other creatures, as the demon powers that had entered them through worship of false gods came out of them. Without Christ we do not have God. Never be satisfied with counterfeit religion. This fact of salvation through Jesus alone should stir our hearts to go and proclaim to the ends of the earth this name which is above *every* name (Philippians 2:9–11), in which there is salvation, healing and true deliverance.

### 6. Without a messenger they will not hear, will not believe, and therefore cannot be saved

In that marvellous book of Romans, the apostle Paul states,

> 'For there is no distinction between Jew and Greek, for the same Lord over all is rich to all who call upon Him. For "whoever calls on the name of the LORD shall be saved."' (Romans 10:12–13)

In the light of such a wonderful revelation, such enormous grace, we can have great confidence in the life-changing power of the gospel we preach. The Greek word for 'salvation', *soteria*, speaks of healing, deliverance, wholeness and protection. The full salvation God offers meets every human need, and is promised to *whomever* calls on the name of the Lord.

However, Paul continues,

> 'How then shall they call on Him in whom they have not believed? And how shall they believe in Him of whom they have not heard? And how shall they hear without a preacher?'
> (Romans 10:14)

Faith comes, not by seeing, or observing, or even experiencing: it comes by *hearing*, and hearing by *the Word of God* (Romans 10:17). Even following the great outpouring of the Spirit at Pentecost, Peter had to get up and preach Christ to them, explaining to them the supernatural phenomenon with which they were being confronted (Acts 2). This combination of Spirit and Word brought with it great results as 3,000 were added to the Church that day.

However, it seems many are willing to pray, many are willing to give, many are willing to do good works (which are all needful), but not so many are willing to *go* and *preach* that saving message of the gospel. It was Jesus who said, *'the harvest truly is plentiful, but the labourers are few!'* (Matthew 9:37). There is apparently no problem with the harvest. The real issue, according to Scripture, is the labourers. Jesus' solution to the scarcity of labourers was two-fold: firstly, to urge the disciples to call out to the Lord of the harvest to thrust out labourers into the harvest; and, secondly, to thrust out the pray-ers (intercessors) themselves, anointing them with divine authority and power to heal the sick and cast out demons, commanding them to go and proclaim that the Kingdom of God is here! Sadly, today, intercession seems to have become somewhat of a specialist ministry, much as the deliverance ministry was perceived to be a few years back. However, neither ministry is seen to be in any way 'specialist' in Scripture, but rather the God-given privilege and responsibility of *every* believer (1 Timothy 2:1–4; Mark 16:17). Would to God that the great army of intercessors being raised up around the world (for which we are all thankful) would not only intercede and overcome in spiritual warfare, but would then *go* forth to reap the harvest for which they have laboured in prayer. We are not called merely to 'bind' the strong man, we are called to 'plunder' his goods (Matthew 12:29).

### 7. *Jesus* commands us to go!

The *Chambers Dictionary* defines the word 'command' as 'to order; to exercise supreme authority over; to demand'. When we consider Jesus' instruction to His disciples, and thus to all believers, in Matthew 28:18–19 and Mark 16:15–18, His words are in 'command form': *'Go therefore and make disciples of all the nations ...'*, *'Go into all the world and preach the gospel to every creature ...'* He begins with a clear statement of His own authority, stating in Matthew 28:18, *'All authority has been given to Me in heaven and on earth'*, then instructing the disciples to go and make disciples of all nations in the light of that authority, assuring them of His immediate presence with them wherever and whenever they go. In the darkest, most godless situations, Jesus is Lord! In the midst of repressive governments, persecuting our fellow believers, in the midst of our hedonistic, secularised Western nations, and in the midst of the most occultic, witchcraft-filled societies, Jesus still has *all* authority in heaven *and on earth*! He, quite unlike the enemy (who can only be in one place at one time), is *omnipresent*, *omniscient* and *omnipotent*, that is, *all* knowing, *all* powerful, *everywhere* at the same time! As His ambassadors, going in His name and under His authority (Matthew 8:5–13: note the connection between understanding authority, faith and healing), we can expect results: salvation, healing, deliverance, and divine protection (Mark 16:15–18). If we want the signs of the Kingdom, we must obey the commands of the King!

### 8. All Israel will be saved when the full number of the Gentiles has come in

It is beyond the scope of this book to undertake an extensive study on the subject of 'Israel', but as far as evangelism is concerned, we are to reach out to the Jewish people just as we are to reach out to the Gentile world (Romans 1:16–17). Furthermore, the promise of God is that when the full number of the Gentiles has come into the Kingdom (God knows those who will respond before they ever hear, but it's our responsibility to go and tell them the gospel), all Israel will be saved (Romans 11:25–26). There is a great movement of prayer for Israel, and we are urged in Psalm 122:6 to pray for the peace of Jerusalem. However, alongside this, one of the greatest things we can do for the Jewish people is to *go* into all the world and preach the gospel. In the purposes of God, when that has been accomplished, as it surely will be (Matthew 24:14, a statement and a promise), *all* Israel will be saved!

### 9. The fields are white unto harvest

In John 4:35 and in Matthew 9:35–38 Jesus says that the fields are white unto harvest. In agricultural understanding, fields are 'white' when they are almost beyond the point of harvesting. It is when the harvest has been left out in the fields, the 'golden' look has all but faded away, and the grain is looking 'husky' and is heavily bending over, ready to die if it is not harvested with the greatest urgency. In human terms, the harvest is the sick, weary and scattered mentioned in Matthew 9:35–36, the poor, broken-hearted, oppressed, bound and blind, to whom Jesus was referring when He spoke of being anointed to proclaim good news, to heal, to set free and to bring recovery of sight (Luke 4:18–19). *We* are the labourers He wants to thrust forth, even into the darkest of places, to bring His light and to rescue those 'trophies of grace', the treasures hidden in the darkness. We must learn not to be put off by the darkness of sin in the lives of those to whom we reach out, knowing that it is the sick who need a doctor and that it is when the darkness is at its darkest that the light shines brightest. Isaiah prophesied that the darkness in the nations would become darker, even 'gross', but the glory of the Lord would rise upon His people, and the nations would come to our light (Isaiah 60:1–2). When we are confronted by a society that is devoid of virtue and filled to the full with perversions, violence and every manner of godlessness, we have a choice to make. We can throw up our arms and give up, we can talk endlessly of the hopeless state of our nation, or we can turn our eyes upon the only One who holds the keys, who is the answer, and see that we stand on the threshold of the Church's greatest opportunity and finest hour. We must choose to behold the Lamb of God who takes *away* the sin of the world (John 1:29). Thus, our faith will be quickened and we will rise to shine His light and take the harvest He has given us.

### 10. The gospel works

It has been my privilege, in the last fourteen years, to preach the gospel in about twenty-seven different nations, sometimes preaching to crowds of up to 200,000 people and at other times sharing the gospel one to one on a doorstep or sitting on a park bench. The simple truth is, whether it's government leaders, businessmen/women, soldiers, prisoners, old people, young people, the gospel works. It is *'the power of God to salvation **for everyone who believes**'* (Romans 1:16). Evangelism is basically a sowing and reaping experience. No farmer would ever sow seed without faith in the seeds' potential to produce a harvest. Jesus said that when seed is sown, *'the earth yields crops **by itself**'* (Mark 4:28). The farmer may not know *how* the seed grows, but he still sows it. All he knows is, *it grows*! Isaiah 55:10–11 says,

> *'For as the rain comes down, and the snow from heaven,*
> *And do not return there,*
> *But water the earth,*
> *And make it bring forth and bud,*
> *That it may give seed to the sower*
> *And bread to the eater,*
> ***So shall My word be*** *that goes forth from My mouth:*
> *It shall **not** return to Me void,*
> ***But it shall*** *accomplish what I please,*
> *And it **shall** prosper in the thing for which I sent it!'*

God sent His Word, as incorruptible seed, to save, heal and deliver (1 Peter 1:23; Psalm 107:20). When it is spoken out of our mouths, since we are His Body (1 Corinthians 12:27), it is spoken out of His mouth. When the prophets spoke in the Old Testament, just because the Word came forth through a human vessel, it did not mean that the words spoken were any less the words of God (2 Peter 1:20–21). Jesus, in the New Testament, is *the Living Word* (John 1:14), and now, as believers, with Christ in us (Colossians 1:27), when we speak His Word, it brings forth salvation (Romans 10:9–10) in the lives of those who receive it. In fact, since faith comes by hearing, *and hearing* by the *Word* of God (Romans 10:17), we can say that the Word has a 'double-barrelled' effect, causing the spiritual ears of the creature to open up and hear the words of his or her Creator, and in so doing to cause faith to come into the heart in the process.

I remember one such occasion in which we were conducting a mission in the south of England. During the day we had been sharing the gospel door to door and on the streets, in preparation for the evening mission services. I was in the middle of communicating the gospel to a woman on the doorstep of her house, when her husband came down the stairs of their home and, swearing at me, slammed the door in my face, making it very clear they did not want anything to do with Jesus. However, believing the Word does not return void, before the door slammed in my face, I said, 'Jesus loves you!' Knowing that such rejection is not personal, I walked away from their home, thanking God for the opportunity I had had to share briefly with them, and prayed that the seed would grow in their hearts. Jesus told us to *'bless those who curse you'* (Matthew 5:44). Such blessing is always so much more powerful than any curse.

Six months later, I returned to conduct some follow-up meetings in the same area. There was a couple singing on the platform and playing an active role in leading the praise and worship that evening who looked very familiar, but I just couldn't place them in my mind. However, at the end of the service, this couple approached me and asked me to forgive them. I said, 'Whatever for?' Their answer was living proof of the incorruptible power of the Word of God. They said, 'Jonathan, we were the couple that swore at you, slammed the door in your face and told you to get off our property! We are so sorry. We watched you from our window, as you walked away, smiling and praying and singing. Looking at each other, we said, "If we swore at him, slammed the door in his face and told him to get off our property, and he's still smiling, tells us 'Jesus loves you', and walks away praying for us, these Christians must have something. We'd better get down to that church and find out what's going on!"' This couple came into the church building in the middle of an Alpha session as new believers were asking questions about what it means to follow Jesus. They quickly gave their lives to Christ and today are active members of that church. There is power in the Word of God!

## 11. *We are hastening the day of His coming*
As we conclude our reasons for evangelising the unsaved, we end

with a most remarkable truth. Realising that we testify of Christ through our words (preaching), works (lifestyle) and wonders (miracles), Peter writes, speaking of the end of all things, and the imminent return of Christ,

> *'Therefore, since all these things will be dissolved, what manner of persons ought you to be in holy conduct and godliness, looking for **and hastening** the day of **God**.'*          (2 Peter 3:11–12)

In Matthew 24:14, Jesus said, *'And this gospel of the kingdom **will** be preached in **all** the world, as a witness to **all** the nations'* [in Greek, *ethnos*, i.e. every ethnic group], *and **then** the end will come.'* He is coming quickly and His reward is with Him. Will you be one of those, looking for and *hastening* the day of His coming, full of the oil of the Holy Spirit, living a godly life, preaching the gospel, using your gifts for His Kingdom, showing His mercy to the poor and needy? Or will you be ashamed at His coming? None of can change our past, but we can all do something about our future. God is more interested in our destiny than He is in our history!

Let's pray:

> Heavenly Father, I thank You for the precious gift of Your Son, Jesus. Thank you that it was Your love that sent Him to die not only for my sins, but for the sins of the whole world. Today, Lord, I hear Your voice, coming to me in the power of Your Word, saying, *'Whom shall I send, and who will go for Us?'* Here I am, Lord, send me. I surrender my life into Your hands as an instrument for Your purpose and Your glory. Please shed abroad Your love in my heart by the power of Your Holy Spirit. Thrust me forth into the harvestfields of Your choosing, with a vision of eternity alive in my heart, equipped with the anointing of Your Spirit, standing in the authority of Christ. Help me minister in Your compassion and grace to a lost and broken world. Your grace is sufficient, Your Presence is with me, and Your Word will not return void!
>
> To You be glory, in Jesus' name, Amen.

### Application

1. (a) Read through the account of Jesus' encounter with the Samaritan woman in John 4:6–42. Consider the setting and progression of their conversation. When was the last time you had a divine appointment with someone unsaved? Make a point of asking God for such appointments on a daily basis, and be sensitive to the Holy Spirit's inward promptings and impressions as you take these God-given opportunities.

   (b) Why did many of the Samaritans believe (v. 39)? How has Jesus changed your life, and in what ways do you now represent a 'living letter of Christ'? Write down your testimony in such a way that it can be communicated in no more than two minutes.

   (c) Write down the names of five people you will commit to pray for (on a regular basis), share your testimony with and personally challenge to give their lives to Christ or invite them to a gathering where such a challenge will be given (set yourself a goal to do this, e.g. six or twelve months).

2. On a scale of 1–10, how would you rate your love for unsaved people? Ask the Father to increase this, and spend some time meditating on the work of the cross as expressed in 2 Corinthians 5:14–21.

3. Would you describe yourself as having 'short-term inspiration' in the gospel, or are you a 'labourer' in His harvest fields? Read over Matthew 25 and consider the following questions:

   - Is my lamp full of the oil of the Holy Spirit? (If not, ask Him to fill you now.)
   - Am I using all my talents/gifts for God, and the extension of His Kingdom?
   - Am I regularly showing His love and compassion to those who are naked/hungry/sick or in prison?

   Turn from past attitudes and inhibitions that have kept you from serving God in fullness, and give yourself in fresh surrender, trusting Him to give all the grace, compassion and ability needed. Renew your commitment to Him today to be a labourer in His great harvest.

# Chapter 2

## The Power to Save

In Romans 1:16, Paul declares,

> 'For I am **not ashamed** of the gospel of Christ, for **it is the power of God to salvation**, for everyone who believes.'

How wonderful it is that we have been sent into all the world to proclaim a message that in and of itself is the power of God to save, heal, deliver and make whole (the Greek word for 'salvation' is *sozo*). *Everyone* who believes it! Many times in gospel campaigns around the world we have seen the Lord healing and delivering people from the oppression of the enemy just as the Word of God is being preached. This should not surprise us and, indeed, should be expected, since it is the Word of God, living and active, sharper than any two-edged sword (Hebrews 4:12), releasing faith in the hearts of those who hear it (Romans 10:17), and healing and deliverance to those who receive it (Psalm 107:20; Proverbs 4:20–22). Not only is the power of God residual/present in the gospel, but God Himself is pleased to save those who believe it, through *the foolishness of preaching* (1 Corinthians 1:21 Amplified Bible). While it has become popular in certain parts of the Church to 'play down' the part that preaching plays in the ministry, the Word of God is plain. God delights to save through the foolishness of preaching. It is a powerful weapon in His hands, foolish to the natural mind, but mighty in the hands of a faith-filled, Holy-Spirit-empowered minister of the gospel (and every believer is a minister; see 1 Peter 2:5). We are called to *preach the gospel*, not just 'give a chat' (Mark 16:15).

Paul commanded Timothy to *'preach the word'* (2 Timothy 4:2). Preaching is *not* teaching (which can hardly be deemed 'foolish', but is much more 'line upon line, precept upon precept'), it is 'heralding, calling out with a clear voice, publicly proclaiming' (definition of Greek *kerusso* in *Strong's Exhaustive Concordance of the Bible*). Preaching is launching out, beyond the words you have prepared either on paper or in your mind, and trusting the Holy Spirit to fill your mouth with His life-giving words that release the power of God into the hearts of the listeners. According to Ephesians 4:29, our very words can *impart grace* (Greek, *charis*: the word used for God's free gift of mercy, undeserved favour, and also the root of 'charismata', the word used for the gift of the Holy Spirit Himself, the gifts of the Spirit, etc.). Our words are carriers of the all-sufficient grace of God that conquers sin and releases the undeserved blessings of God in the lives of those who receive it, *so preach the Word, and expect results!*

## The Message

When Peter preached on the Day of Pentecost, three thousand were saved. When Philip preached in Samaria, demons were cast out, many who were paralysed were healed, and there was great joy in that city. When Paul preached all over Asia and into Europe, thousands were saved, mighty signs and wonders were accomplished, and many new churches were planted. Acts 8 tells us that following the great persecution against the Church that arose in Jerusalem after the death of Stephen, the believers were scattered, and they preached everywhere they went. (It is interesting to note that Philip, who was one of the 'seven' chosen to serve at tables in Acts 6:5, was not recognised as an evangelist when the move of God broke out in Samaria through his ministry. He was just one of those who had been scattered by the persecution, preaching as they went. It's not until Acts 21:8 that we learn that the Church later recognised him as an evangelist. Function precedes office. Just step out and start preaching the gospel where you are and see what God will do with *you!*)

I remember preaching in a city notorious for kidnapping,

murder and prostitution. We were preaching in the open plaza, where many of our listeners had guns strapped to their waists or thighs. When I would say something they didn't want to hear, they would reach for their guns. That would make me preach even more fervently and the anointing would get stronger, then the guns would go back in their holders. Five hundred people surrendered their lives to Christ each night in the open air as God confirmed His Word with signs following! Praise God! There is something about the message of the Good News which is so compelling, so powerful, so divine, that even in its delivery a preacher is set free from fear and caused to rise above the temporal threats of men and the opposition of the powers of darkness.

It is always best to let Scripture be its own interpreter, so let's turn to 1 Corinthians 15:1–5 where Paul clearly lays out the message he preached that changed lives then, and changes lives now.

> '*Moreover, brethren, I declare to you* **the gospel** *which I preached to you, which also you received and in which you stand, by which also you are saved, if you hold fast that word which I preached to you – unless you believed in vain. For I delivered to you first of all that which I also received* [from God: Galatians 1:11–12]: *that Christ died for our sins according to the Scriptures, and that He was buried, and that He rose again the third day according to the Scriptures, and that He was seen . . . '* (1 Corinthians 15:1–5)

Let's look at this gospel, this 'Good News' by which we are saved, in more detail.

## 1. Christ died *for* our sins

Christ's death was different from every other death that has ever taken place. He didn't die for a political agenda; He didn't even die for a 'religious' belief; He died *for* our sins. It was not the horrendous physical abuse of His beatings and whipping (in the process of which many men died) that killed Him, nor even the excruciating agony of being nailed to and hung on a cross. In John 10:17–18, Jesus said,

'... *I lay down My life that I may take it again. No one takes it from Me, but I lay it down of Myself. I have power to lay it down, and I have power to take it again. This command I have received from My Father.*'

Not until Jesus 'gave up His Spirit' could He die, for there was no death in Him! Romans 6:23 tells us that *'the wages of sin is death'*. Christ never sinned, so He did not need to die. Peter, preaching on the Day of Pentecost, said,

> *'Him, being delivered* **by the determined purpose and fore-knowledge of God***, you have taken by lawless hands, have crucified, and put to death; whom God raised up, having loosed the pains of death, because* **it was not possible that He should be held by it.**' (Acts 2:23–24)

Christ died as a *substitute*, not a martyr! He prophesied His own death *and* His own resurrection (Matthew 16:21). It was the plan of God to redeem and restore mankind to Himself. His death on our behalf and subsequent resurrection were prophesied throughout the Old Testament, Isaiah 53 being perhaps the best-known passage. Philippians 2:8–9 tells us that,

> '... *He humbled Himself and became obedient to the point of death, even the death of the cross.* **Therefore** *God also has* **highly** *exalted Him and given Him* **the name which is above every name.**'

This message of substitution, of a divine exchange, is absolutely unique amongst the religions of the world. That the Creator Himself (see John 1:1, 3) would die in the place of the creatures He had made, for the sins they had committed *against Him*, is unfathomable grace, immeasurable love! A Muslim once said to me, 'Jon, what you are saying is very much like Islam, for Mohammed said that if you truly repent, then God would forgive you.' I responded, 'That's all very well, but there is a problem. The wages of sin is *not* repentance, but death. Repentance is a response to God's grace, but it is not the price for sin. Since God is eternally just, until the price for that sin is paid, there can be no forgiveness. Either someone has got to love you enough to die for you, in your place, paying the price for your sin, or else you are going to have to pay it yourself! And the price is death – not only physical death but eternal death. Furthermore, it can't just be anyone dying for you, it has to be someone who is absolutely perfect, otherwise it would be sin paying for sin, and that isn't substitution, that isn't justice.' Seeing that he was impacted by the truth of God's Word, I added, 'And you and I both know that neither Allah nor Mohammed died *for* you, did they? But Jesus, the perfect, blameless Son of God, did exactly that.' Within minutes he bowed his head and gave his life to Christ! The message of the cross *is* the power of God (1 Corinthians 1:18).

Christ's death on our behalf was a substitutionary sacrifice, not only dealing eternally with our sin, but also with its consequences, thus bringing the salvation of God to bear on every issue of life that human beings could ever face. This 'divine exchange' can be summarised as follows:

- Jesus was punished *that* we might be forgiven (Isaiah 53:4–5).

- Jesus was wounded *that* we might be healed (Isaiah 53:4–5).

- Jesus was made sin with our sinfulness *that* we might be made righteous with His righteousness (Isaiah 53:10; 2 Corinthians 5:21).

- Jesus died our death *that* we might receive His life (Hebrews 2:9).

- Jesus was made a curse *that* we might enter into His blessing (Galatians 3:13–14).

- Jesus endured our poverty *that* we might share His abundance (2 Corinthians 8:9; 9:8).

- Jesus bore our shame *that* we might share His glory (Matthew 27:35–36; Hebrews 2:9; 12:2).

- Jesus endured our rejection *that* we might have His acceptance with the Father (Matthew 27:46–51; Ephesians 1:5–6).

- Jesus was cut off by death *that* we might be joined to God eternally (Isaiah 53:8; 1 Corinthians 6:17).

- Our old man was put to death in Him *that* the new man might come to life in us (Romans 6:6; Colossians 3:9–10).

Wherever and whenever this message is preached, the power of God is manifested to confirm it with signs following. Since forgiveness, healing, righteousness, life, blessing, abundance and all the other wonderful things Jesus died to give us were His idea, not ours, we can expect Him to do those very things in confirmation of His Word as we go forth obediently to preach it!

## 2. He was buried

Burial is legal evidence of death. It is the end (at least physically speaking – until the resurrection at the end of the age!). It was the normal practice for Roman soldiers after a certain period to break the legs of those they crucified so that they could no longer lift themselves up on the cross, and would thus die of asphyxiation. In the case of Jesus they were surprised that He had died so quickly. Many men lived on for days, some even for weeks. However, Jesus died with a purpose, bearing the sins of the whole world on His shoulders. He gave up His spirit, and taking His last breath before dying He cried, *'It is finished!'* (John 19:30). We are also told in 2 Corinthians 5:14 that, *'If One died for all, then all died!'* You and I are included in that *'all'*. Romans 6:3–4 declares,

> *'... as many of us as were baptized into Christ Jesus were baptized into His death ... Therefore we were buried with Him through baptism into death, that just as Christ was raised from the dead by the glory of the Father, even so we also should walk in newness of life.'*

Sin has no power over a man who has died! Your sin was buried with Christ: your curse, your sickness, your poverty, your rejection, your shame, your death. These glorious words from Galatians 2:20 ring in my heart,

> *'I have been crucified with Christ; it is no longer I who live, but Christ lives in me; and the life which I now live in the flesh I live by faith in the Son of God, who loved me and gave Himself for me.'*

This is the awesome truth of the substitutionary work of Christ. God did not only deal with sin, He dealt with the sinner. He not only dealt with my offences, He dealt with me. The old nature is gone; a new life has come! I remember having the privilege of baptising a terrorist who had come to Christ in an evangelistic mission with which we had been involved in Asia. He had been personally responsible for the deaths of many innocent people. As I took him down into the waters of baptism, God gave me a vision of blood coming off the man's hands. In response to my question, 'What's that, Lord?', God spoke ever so clearly into my heart: 'It is the blood of all the lives he has taken. Never again will I require it from his hands.' Today that man is a pastor in the Philippines, giving life instead of taking it. What a mighty God we serve!

## 3. He rose again

In Paul's letter to the Romans we are told that Jesus was *'declared to be the Son of God with power according to the Spirit of holiness, by the resurrection from the dead'* (1:4). Paul goes on to tell us that Christ was delivered up because of our transgressions, and was raised for (or, because) of our justification (4:25). We are saved by believing that God raised Jesus from the dead and confessing Him as Lord (Romans 10:9). It is the indisputable evidence that Jesus is who He says He is. He fulfilled the ancient prophecies concerning Himself, rising from the dead never to die again. He demonstrated His complete victory over death, hell and the grave. His resurrection is the evidence that God accepted His substitutionary death on the cross on our behalf as the full price for our sins past, present and future, and now, whoever believes on Him shall not perish, but have eternal life. It is also the evidence and assurance that just as Christ has been raised from the dead, so also will all those who believe on Him rise from the dead, at His coming, with the self-same resurrection bodies as He has, never to die again (1 Corinthians 15:20–23).

It is a concerning thing in some of our modern gospel preaching today that the resurrection of Christ from the dead is not preached as regularly and fervently as it should be. In 1 Corinthians 15:17 Paul declares plainly,

> *'And if Christ is not risen, your faith is futile; you are still in your sins!'*

It's interesting to note that Paul did *not* say, 'If Christ did not die for you on the cross, your faith is futile', or that we are saved by believing Christ died for our sins on the cross. While all that is gloriously true (i.e. Christ *did* die for our sins on the cross), Paul states that we are saved by believing in our hearts that *God raised Jesus from the dead and confessing Him as Lord* (Romans 10:9–10). I have sometimes sat through a presentation of the gospel, seen an appeal for salvation made, people respond and pray a prayer of commitment to Christ, without the resurrection of Christ being once proclaimed, nor any confession of faith concerning His resurrection being made in 'the sinner's prayer'. Then we wonder why the results from such outreaches are so minimal in terms of ongoing discipleship! If the resurrection was not proclaimed, nor believed in the heart, we can quite confidently say, from these scriptures, that there could have been no salvation in the hearts of those who responded. Those of us who preach the gospel are responsible to make sure we communicate the true and full gospel of Christ, and therefore give everyone who hears the greatest opportunity to be genuinely saved.

The resurrection of Christ from the dead sets Jesus apart from every religious leader, cult figure or guru who has ever lived on this planet. He is the unique and undisputed Son of God and Saviour of the world. He is Lord and Christ! We will look at the resurrection of Christ in terms of its implications for our new identity and authority in Him in the next chapter, but for now let us simply rejoice in the truth that our old life died in Christ and we are raised together with Him into a new life of victory, freedom and dominion over all the powers of darkness. Christ's victory was so conclusive that the Apostle Paul declares that He made 'a public spectacle' of the principalities and powers (Colossians 2:15), and, *'had they known, they would not have crucified the Lord of glory'* (1 Corinthians 2:8). In his vision of Jesus on the Isle of Patmos, John heard Him say,

> *'I am He who lives, and was dead, and behold, I am alive for evermore. Amen. And I have the keys* [authority] *of Hades and of Death.'*                           (Revelation 1:18)

Jesus is 'the seed' that crushed the serpent's head (Genesis 3:15), and, still today, it is *through us*, the Body of Christ, that Satan experiences the crushing pain of his defeat in the name of Jesus Christ (Romans 16:20).

## 4. He was seen

Yes, this is part of the gospel! Christ was seen. Four times in four verses Paul declares, *'He was seen'* (1 Corinthians 5–8). Although it is true that Jesus Himself said to doubting Thomas, *'because you have seen Me, you have believed. Blessed are those who have not seen and yet have believed'* (John 20:29), Jesus revealed Himself alive to His followers after the resurrection, giving them many infallible proofs and teaching them concerning the Kingdom of God (Acts 1:3). Jesus always confirms His Word, His promises, with signs following. Indisputable, infallible signs (Mark 16:20). He knows that there are many who *'unless* [they] *see signs and wonders* [they] *will by no means believe'* (John 4:48). And He wants them to believe.

As I have gone around the world, preaching the gospel, the Lord has always, in one way or another, confirmed His word with signs following. These signs have varied from the deaf hearing, cripples walking, demons being cast out, etc., to unusual manifestations of His power and provision (sometimes even multiplying money in our wallets as extra finance was needed in evangelistic ministry or giving to the poor), and even to times when He has chosen to reveal Himself in such a way that people have seen Him amongst us. For personal encouragement, let me share one among the many such accounts.

Before going to Rwanda, I was told prophetically that the things I had heard about but not yet seen, I would see. What happened while ministering on a hot afternoon up on a mountainside near Gisenyi came right into that category. Many had already surrendered their lives to Christ amongst the 5,000 people gathered together to hear the gospel that day. I had prayed, asking the Lord to move in power, healing the sick that were amongst us, and a number of people had come forward to testify of the healing they had experienced in those moments.

Suddenly, from the back of the crowd, a woman came forward shouting and praising, her face shining with the glory of God upon her. As she told the excited crowd what had happened, my interpreter translated, 'She came to this meeting virtually completely blind, helped by her friends. However, as you prayed over the crowd, she saw a man standing in front of her, dressed in white. She knew it was Jesus. A sensation of heat went through her body and her eyes were perfectly opened. She can now see.' Needless to say, there was great rejoicing in all that the Lord had done amongst us that day.

The apostle Paul testifies in 1 Corinthians 15:10 that *'by the grace of God, I am what I am, and His grace toward me was not in vain'*. Salvation is a miracle of God's grace that takes place in our hearts when we believe in Jesus Christ and what He has done for us in His death, burial and resurrection. It changes us completely from the inside-out. It is what Jesus called *'the gospel of the kingdom'* (Matthew 24:14), the Good News that there is 'another King'. We were all born into Satan's kingdom because of the sin of our forefather Adam, but we do not have to be under the rule of this enemy who kills, robs and destroys our lives anymore (John 10:10), but through faith in Christ we can be born again into a new Kingdom. This is the message that must be believed, lived and preached.

In summary:

- The Kingdom *has* come. Jesus *has* provided salvation, and through faith in Him we *have* been saved, our spirits *have* been born again.

- The Kingdom *is here*. Jesus dwells within us by the power of His Holy Spirit to effect all the benefits of salvation in our lives, to comfort, help, heal and guide us, and empower us to testify to the world about Him. We are *being* saved as our souls are restored, our minds renewed, and our bodies offered to Him as a living sacrifice.

- The Kingdom *is coming*. Jesus is returning, physically, to this earth, and the time is short. Every eye will see Him; every knee will bow and confess that *Jesus Christ is Lord!* We will receive resurrection bodies, the living and the dead will both be eternally judged, and we will reign forever with Him.

- Christ has died, Christ is risen, Christ will come again!

Let's pray:

Father, I thank You today that You have saved and delivered me from the power of sin and darkness. I thank You that this same Jesus who lived and walked among us, healing, forgiving, and changing lives, died for me, rose again, and now lives in my heart. I yield to Your Spirit within me, Lord. I submit to Your call. I thank You that You have given me the one and only message that can change the world today, and I will be faithful to communicate it everywhere I go, and at every opportunity. Help me to present the full gospel, Lord, the Truth that sets people free. Help me never to compromise, never to bow out to the fear of man, but always to be bold for You. Thank You that You are with me always, even to the end of the age, that You will confirm Your Word with signs accompanying it, and that You will reward me on that Day when You come again. May I be found faithful to the end.

In Jesus' name, Amen.

### Application

1. In what ways have you experienced the truth of Romans 1:16 in your own life and ministry?

2. Should we expect supernatural results from our preaching? Study Psalm 107:20, Isaiah 55:10–11, Mark 16:20, Romans 10:17, 1 Corinthians 1:21.

3. Summarise the gospel (1 Corinthians 15:1–5). When you present the gospel to people, either individually or corporately, do you clearly proclaim the *full* gospel? Make a fresh commitment today always to do so.

# Chapter 3

# The Believer's Authority

We were preaching the gospel all around Slovakia in Eastern Europe. During the daytime we were singing and preaching on the streets, and in the evenings we were conducting evangelistic/ healing meetings in each of the towns in which we ministered. The Lord had been working with us performing a number of miracles, opening some deaf ears, lengthening legs that were too short (a condition that causes back problems), healing internal illnesses, etc. However, I was greatly dissatisfied, seeing some people leaving the meetings still in their wheelchairs, or walking on crutches. I gathered the team around me and told them, 'I am deeply dissatisfied. Ephesians 1:3 tells us that we have been blessed with every spiritual blessing in the heavenly places in Christ! The Greek word for "spiritual" in this instance is the same word used in 1 Corinthians 12:1 for "spiritual gifts", which includes gifts of healings, working of miracles, and special faith. These gifts are included in the spiritual blessings that are ours in Christ, which means we have them *now*. However, they are *"in the heavenly places in Christ"*. We are going to rise up in our spirits, and take hold of these blessings in the heavenly places by praying in the Spirit [tongues], confessing the Word and praising God for these miracles until they manifest amongst us. Jesus said, *"the kingdom of heaven suffers violence, and the violent **take it by force"**.* James said, *"The earnest, heartfelt* [fervent, NKJV], *contin- ued prayer of a righteous man* [this is prayer with energy!] *makes tremendous power available, dynamic in its working"*[1] Everything is available, and the people we are ministering to don't know how

---

[1] Matthew 11:12; James 5:16 Amplified, with author's added comments.

to reach out in faith to God, but we do. Therefore, increase your praying in tongues, increase your intake of the Word (which increases your faith), increase your praise, and step out in Spirit-led, reckless faith!' To cut a long story short, the release of the miraculous amongst us was multiplied many times over. Cripples walked, the deaf heard, the blind saw, growths disappeared, and hundreds came to Christ.

I want you to know that this same power is available to you as a believer in Jesus Christ. It is *not* the realm of the specialist: it is the realm of the believer. Such demonstration is normal New Testament Christianity, and works in any culture, any nation, where believers believe and are prepared to put action to their faith, releasing God's supernatural power into the natural world to bring change and restoration. This very normal activity of heaven (from God's perspective), we call 'miracles', and He does them through our faith.

### 'The works that I do, he will do also'

In John 14:12, Jesus categorically states, *'he who believes in Me, the works that I do, he will do also; and greater works than these will he do, because I go to My Father.'* This is not a promise, it is a statement of fact. He continues, 'And **whatever** you demand [emphasis of the Greek] **in My name**, that will I do, that the Father may be glorified in the Son' (John 14:13). Whereas in John 16:23–24 Jesus tells us about prayer *to the Father*, which is petition, here Jesus is speaking about making demands of the enemy. Consider Jesus' prayers for the sick: 'stretch out your arm', 'rise up and walk', 'receive your sight'. No evidence of a petition to the Father there! Jesus petitioned His Father in private, and released what He received from the Father in public. We are to do the same.

When we command the enemy, in Jesus' name, to release those whom he has held captive with sickness, demonic oppression, fear, etc., Jesus is right there with us, in the power of the Holy Spirit, to enforce the *command* of faith given and set the captive free. Mark 16:17–18 further attests to the believer's right to exercise such authority,

> *'And these signs* **will** *follow* **those who believe** [lit. the believ-
> ing ones]*:* ***In My name*** *they* **will** *cast out demons; they* **will**
> *speak with new tongues … they* **will** *lay hands on the sick, and*
> *they* **will** *recover.'*

The clear testimony of Scripture is that the authority to perform
miracles *in His name* is given to those who *believe*. These are days
when the harvest is so great that we *must* envision, equip, and
release *every* believer to be an effective harvester in the Kingdom.
It is the season when God is raising up His *Church* – not just
individuals within her, but the corporate Body of Christ. Anything less will not be sufficient to gather the harvest appointed
for us!

I grew up in the United Kingdom, in a Christian family, at a
time now known around the world as the 'Charismatic Renewal'.
They were powerful days of wonderful worship, great demonstrations of God's power in gifts of the Spirit, and a growing
revelation of the priesthood of *all* believers. Growing up in such
an environment, I was baptised in the Holy Spirit at a young age,
speaking in tongues and experiencing the gifts and presence of
the Holy Spirit on a regular basis. I knew what it was to respond
to the Spirit, but I did not know whether the Spirit of God would
respond to me! I didn't know then what I know now – that the
Spirit of God is *always* ready to demonstrate His grace and power
to and through the person who believes. That if we will draw
near to God in faith, then He will draw near to us. In Galatians
3:5, Paul asks,

> *'Therefore He who supplies the Spirit to you, and works miracles*
> *among you, does He do it by the works of the law, or by the*
> *hearing of faith?'*

The answer is obvious. God supplies His Spirit to us, and works
miracles amongst us, not because we have lived a perfect life (to
the letter of the law), but because we believe His Word. When I
heard the simple truth that I am who God says I am, and I can do
what God says I can do, I just started to act on it with simple
faith, sharing the gospel with people everywhere I went, and
praying for the sick. On the streets, at school, in the trains – God

did miracles, healed sick people, and saved the lost. I didn't know what an evangelist was, I just thought this is what believers are supposed to do. I was just obeying the word to go into all the world and preach the gospel, expecting that if I did my part, then He would do His and these signs would follow. And they did.

## Jesus commissioned 'babes'

In Luke 10 we have the account of Jesus sending out the seventy-two to go ahead of Him and prepare the way in the towns where He was about to go. They were sent out with specific orders (amongst other things) to heal the sick, and tell them, *'The kingdom of God has come near to you.'* What is remarkable about this account is the level of 'maturity' recognised by Jesus in those He was sending out to represent Him. In verse 3 He described them as 'lambs' (not even full-grown 'sheep'), and when they came back rejoicing, stating how even the demons were subject to them *in His name*, Jesus *'rejoiced in the Spirit'* (this was obviously a great delight to all three members of the Godhead) – the Greek text suggests 'shouting and leaping for joy', proclaiming,

> *'I thank You, Father, Lord of heaven and earth, that You have hidden these things from the wise and prudent and revealed them to babes. Even so, Father, for so it seemed good in Your sight.'*
>
> (Luke 10:21)

Jesus said that He saw Satan fall like lightning from heaven (his place of dominion in the 'heavenlies' over the area where the disciples had gone to minister). Jesus used spiritual 'babes' to topple Satan's rule in the heavenly realms over an area, as they went out with imparted authority and anointing from Him to heal the sick and proclaim the immediate presence of God's Kingdom. What is further, His prayer of rejoicing that followed the event underlines that God delights to use the 'babes' who are so desperately dependent on Him, and also finds it good to 'hide' the secrets of His power from the 'wise' and 'prudent'. We would do well to learn from this. Those who humble themselves in childlike dependence and faith, find themselves in a place of tremendous power when stepping out in simple obedience to the Master's word.

I remember being stopped at a military checkpoint in Uganda by a nine-year-old boy-soldier with an automatic rifle in his hand. I couldn't help but be impressed by the fact that, without his arms, it would have been a fairly simple task to overpower him – had I wanted to! However, therein lay the problem! He was armed! He would only have had to pull the trigger of his rifle and I would have been 'promoted to glory'. The enemy is not so concerned by who we are: he is concerned by who we are 'in Christ', that we have *'weapons of warfare'* that are *'mighty in God for pulling down strongholds'* (2 Corinthians 10:4). When we are submitted to God, and take the mighty weapons of the name of Jesus, the blood of Jesus and the Word of God, and release them through the confession of our lips, the high praises of God, and the command of faith, the enemy has to flee in terror (James 4:7).

When you consider the scriptural definition of a 'spiritual babe' (1 John 2:12–13 – one who knows his sins are forgiven and that God is his Father), the reality of the authority we have been *given* in Christ becomes even more exciting. John said,

> *'You are of God, **little children**, and have overcome them* [the anti-Christ spirit], **because** *He who is in you is greater than he who is in the world.'* (1 John 4:4)

It is these weapons that cast down 'arguments' and every 'high thing' that exalts itself against the knowledge of God, bringing every thought into captivity to the obedience of Christ. But before we use these weapons to overcome the works of the enemy in the lives of others, we must learn to use them first against the strongholds the enemy seeks to establish in our own minds. If we are to live our lives in effective service for the Kingdom of God, thoughts of unbelief, of fear, anxiety, impurity or pride must be cast down and made captive to the obedience of Christ. Spiritual battles are won or lost in your mind! If the Spirit of God prompts you to go and say, 'Stand up and walk' to a crippled person in a wheelchair, for example, and the thought comes to you, 'But what if he doesn't get healed?', what you do with that thought will determine whether or not the victory of Jesus will be seen at that time. Through the years I have learned to 'reverse it to disperse it'. In such situations, learn to answer, 'But what if He does? And what's more, He will, because Jesus said, "Whatever I ask in His name, He will do it!"' Then act on your faith and see the power of God manifest! It's true in ministry situations, standing in faith for your own health or finances, overcoming temptations, in relationships, in fact in just about every area of life you care to mention. Amos 3:3 says, *'Can two walk together, unless they are agreed?'* Learn to agree with God – in your thoughts, your words, your deeds. When you do, there is no blockage to the full flow of His authority in your life, and you will see His grace and power operating mightily in your life and ministry.

## Authority: a definition

Jesus said,

> *'Behold, I give you the authority to trample on serpents and scorpions, and over **all** the power of the enemy, and nothing shall by any means hurt you. Nevertheless, do not rejoice in this, that the spirits are subject to you, but rather rejoice because your names are written in heaven.'* (Luke 10:19–20)

I am talking here about the authority given by Christ to *every* believer, not the issue of leadership authority which is a totally different subject. Two points are especially worthy of note (particularly in the current climate of so much teaching on 'spiritual warfare'): firstly, every individual believer is given authority over *all* the power of the enemy; secondly, we have a promise from God that *'nothing shall by any means hurt you.'* We are not to believe in 'counter-attack' lest the enemy uses our own faith in his attacks to open the door for his oppressions. I am *not* advocating a 'light' approach to facing our enemy but, without question, our faith and respect must be more in the Word of God and the Jesus who saved us and defeated all the powers of hell, than in the enemy who threatens us. We need to ensure our faith is in the right place before we ever engage the enemy! After all, it is the shield of *faith* that extinguishes *all* the flaming arrows of the evil one (Ephesians 6:16).

Wherever we are pioneering with the gospel, there is spiritual opposition to overcome. On one occasion in Rwanda, we were holding seminars for leaders during the day, to equip them in the gifts of the Spirit, and doing an evangelistic campaign in the evenings. We had seen hundreds coming to Christ, and a few minor healings, but nothing greater in terms of the miraculous (i.e. that would make a great impact), and we wondered where the opposition we were experiencing was coming from. Then one day, while walking through the town, we were confronted by a witch who began to scream her curses at us. Realising what was happening, I started to move towards her, addressing her in the name of Jesus. She began to run away, with me in hot pursuit, and then she vanished into thin air in front of me! Now we realised where our real battle lay. We phoned the church back home for supporting prayer and, taking our authority in the name of Jesus, spent most of the evening in warfare prayer. When the praises of God began to break forth within us, accompanied by a great sense of release and freedom in the Spirit, we knew we had the breakthrough. The following day, in the crusade, we had our first major miracle when a boy born blind in one eye received his sight. From that point on, the miracles flowed, the meetings took off (Jesus even appeared to someone in the crowds, and the person was instantly healed), and over two thousand people came to Christ. Glory to God!

*The Chambers Dictionary* defines authority as 'the lawful right to enforce obedience or power'. Since Jesus' finished work at Calvary and His victorious resurrection (after which He revealed Himself to His disciples, saying, '***All*** *authority has been given to* ***Me*** *in heaven* ***and on earth***. ***Go therefore*** *and make disciples of* ***all*** *the nations ... ',* Matthew 28:18–19), we have been commissioned by Christ to proclaim and enforce (spiritually) His dominion to the ends of the earth.

David said, *'power belongs to God'* (Psalm 62:11). In Acts 1:8 we are told, *'You shall* ***receive*** *power when the Holy Spirit has come upon you'* (the Greek word for 'power' is *dunamis*: ability, i.e. of God, and is used of 'mighty works', 'miracles', etc.). For us to exercise

His power we must be authorised by Him to do so. This is what it means to pray or minister *in His name*. It is according to His nature, His will, with His backing or authorisation. It is like having the legal power of attorney. We can do whatever He has said we can do with His resources, with the only limit being (1) the level of His resources – unlimited, and (2) the boundaries of what He has said we can, and must do.

The Greek word for 'authority' is *exousia*, meaning 'freedom of action, the right to act'. When used of God it is absolute and unrestricted. When used of man, it is always delegated.

Whatever His Word tells us to do, we can do. Whatever His Spirit tells us to do we can do (and it will be in agreement with the written Word), and we can expect Him to back up our words and actions of faith with the power that He promises in His Word.

## Principles that govern the release of divine authority through the Church

It is fair to say that God, in His integrity, operates by the same principles revealed in His Word that He has told us to live by. He is the Creator, we are the created, and we can only operate in His authority to the degree to which we live under His authority. Just as the first Adam was God's under-ruler in the earth, Jesus, the last Adam (1 Corinthians 15:45), had to live and minister as a man under God, defeating the enemy as a man, thus restoring to man his proper place as God's under-ruler in the earth, through the redemptive work of Christ. It was the Seed of the woman that crushed the serpent's head (Genesis 3:15; note: headship speaks of authority, cf. 1 Corinthians 11:3). Jesus, as the last Adam, brought an end to the domination of sin, thus removing Satan's only legal hold upon fallen humanity. As the Second Man, He is the beginning of the New Creation of God, of which you and I through Christ are a part. This New Creation will culminate in the creation of a new heaven, a new earth, the eternal removal of Satan from human contact (and his subsequent eternal torment), and the immediate dwelling of God with human beings (Revelation 20–21). Until that time, it is our task, as believers in Jesus Christ, to enforce His victory through the gospel to the ends of the earth – to occupy until He comes, living for the salvation of the lost, and the bringing to full maturity of the Bride of Christ, the Church. Our authority to minister as He ministered must flow out of the same principles by which He lived and operated.

Let's consider these principles and then take them to heart, and believe and walk as He walked!

### 1. *Jesus' authority flowed from* His identity

In John 14:10–11 Jesus stated that the words He spoke and the miracles He performed flowed from the dynamic of His identity and relationship to the Father: *'I am in the Father and the Father in Me'*. Our authority flows from exactly the same principle. We are 'in Christ' (1 Corinthians 1:30), and Christ is in us (Colossians 1:27). His victory is our victory (Colossians 2:11–15). We are raised with Christ, seated with Christ, in a place of total dominion over principalities and powers (Ephesians 2:6; 1:21–23).

### 2. *Jesus' authority flowed from* His walk

Jesus said,

> *'... the Son can do nothing of Himself, but what He sees the Father do ... As I hear I judge; and my judgment is righteous, because I do not seek my own will, but the will of the Father who sent Me.'* (John 5:19, 30)

The centurion in Matthew 8:5–13 understood this principle, when he said, *'I, **also**, am a man under authority, having soldiers under me. And I say to this one, "Go," and he goes ... '* He recognised that Jesus was operating under the Father's authority, and when Jesus commanded sickness to go, it had to leave as if the Father Himself had spoken. We operate under the same principle, and it is a principle that releases great faith (Matthew 8:10)! However, we must understand that we cannot pray effectively with a guilty conscience (1 John 3:21–22), and we cannot successfully resist the devil, if we do not first submit to God (James 4:7). But if we are submitted to God, declaring His Words after Him, we will see the enemy flee from us just as if he were fleeing from God Himself!

### 3. Jesus' authority flowed from His call

In John 8:14 Jesus expressed His right to give testimony because He knew where He had come from, and He knew where He was going. Throughout Scripture, names were given as expressions of divinely inspired callings, destinies and purpose (consider Abraham: Father of a Multitude, Genesis 17:5; Israel: Prince with God, Genesis 32:28). Jesus' name, given by God, through the angel Gabriel means 'God is salvation' (Matthew 1:21). His calling was to seek and save that which is lost, to preach good news to the poor, heal the broken-hearted, proclaim liberty to the captives and recovery of sight to the blind, to proclaim the acceptable year of the Lord (Luke 4:18–19).

In John 20:21 Jesus said, *'As the Father has sent Me, I also send you.'* In Matthew 28:18–19, He declared,

> *'All authority has been given to Me in heaven and on earth. Go therefore, and make disciples of all the nations, baptizing them in the name of the Father and of the Son and of the Holy Spirit, teaching them to observe all things that I have commanded you; and lo, I am with you always, even to the end of the age.'*

God has not called us to be 'spiritual pacifists', but much rather 'spiritual militants', activists in the Kingdom of God, forcefully advancing the reign of our King. He has given us a new identity, a new life, a new calling and purpose, with the authority to back it up!

In closing this section of *Militant Christianity*, I would like to share with you just one of the miracles that took place in Slovakia, on that mission trip to which I referred right at the beginning of the chapter. It illustrates the impact that is made when we follow in the footsteps of the One who came to *'destroy the works of the devil'* (1 John 3:8).

We were in Liptovsky Mikulas, preaching the gospel in the 'house of culture'. The night before many gypsies had come forward to surrender their lives to Christ, but their conduct after the gathering represented a total denial of the profession they had made in the meeting! I was praying, asking the Lord to really 'break out' in their lives and show them the reality of what they had been into and the need of true repentance. The following night, I addressed them when they came forward in response to the appeal again. After rebuking them for their hypocritical behaviour (while assuring them of our love for them!), I got off the platform and walked amongst them, laying hands on each and every one of them, commanding the enemy to loose his grip on their lives. Immediately, one teenage girl fell on the floor convulsing and screaming. My instinctive reaction was to command the demons to come out of her, but seeing the opportunity for a powerful object lesson, I called all the gypsies round to watch. As they looked on with a sense of fear and great astonishment, I asked them, 'Does she do this often?' They answered, 'No!' Realising I now had their full attention, I told them, 'What you are looking at is the demonic powers that are present in the immorality, lying, theft and occult activities many of you are involved in. If you want to become like this, just stay the way you are. But now you will see the power of Jesus Christ to defeat the powers of darkness, and you decide whom you will serve!' After commanding the demons to leave her in Jesus' name, the girl shrieked and fell limp on the floor. Suddenly she came around, her face shining with the joy and freedom only Jesus can give. She was soon baptised in the Holy Spirit and restored to her family, a free girl! What followed was glorious, as many of the gypsies truly repented, and two days later were baptised in water, giving their lives fully to Christ.

*Remember*: You are who God says you are, and you can do what God says you can do. Rise up and take your place in God's great end-time army. The harvest fields of your community, your nation, and indeed your world are waiting for you to bring the freedom, the grace, and the healing power of God in Jesus' name.

Let's pray:

> Father, I thank You today that I am Your son/daughter, an heir of God, and a joint-heir with Jesus Christ. I praise You for the great privilege You have given me to serve You by living, proclaiming and demonstrating Your Kingdom everywhere I go. Thank You that for every commission You've given me, You have also given me the authority and

power to do what You say. I believe Your Word concerning my new identity in Christ and right now, receiving Your authority, I embrace my destiny, living all my days to honour and glorify Your Holy Name. Amen.

## Application

1. In your Bible, start underlining in different colours the verses that tell you who God says you are, and the things He says you can do. Then spend some time over each verse, verbally repeating the truth in personal form, and thanking Him for it. For example, 'Thank you, Father, that I can do all things through Christ who strengthens me' (Philippians 4:13). Make this a regular spiritual exercise, and watch your faith grow.

2. Do you have 'strongholds' in your thinking that need to be brought into submission to Christ (2 Corinthians 10:3–5)? If so, spend some time now renouncing them and declaring the truth of God's Word that sets you free. Where necessary, repent, forgive others and embrace His Word as the *final* word on that issue.

3. Spend some time meditating on the authority of Jesus, and the place of dominion we have been given 'in Him' (Colossians 2:11–15; Ephesians 1:21–23; 2:6; Philippians 2:9–11; Matthew 28:18–19).

4. Summarise the calling of Jesus as revealed in Matthew 1:21, Luke 4:18–19, and 1 John 3:8. How should we as believers, following in His footsteps, be leading our lives? Write down three ways in which you can practically implement the call of Jesus in your life, and start today to live it out.

# Chapter 4

# Blood and Fire!

'Blood and fire', the watchwords of the Salvation Army, were the basic necessities for effective ministry in evangelism in William Booth's army. A clear testimony of salvation from sin, and a burning passion for the lost ignited by the Holy Spirit. They knew that the Holy Spirit was poured out on the Day of Pentecost because the blood of Jesus had been accepted in the Holy of Holies as the once-for-all eternal sacrifice for our sin. They knew the Spirit answers to the Blood, and they were no strangers to His power. Elijah Cadman, one of Booth's Salvationists, had such an anointing for preaching the gospel that when people, under a great weight of conviction, could not move off their seats to get down to 'the mercy seat' (in response to an appeal for salvation), the Holy Spirit would 'pick them up' and carry them over several rows of seats (in mid-air!) and drop them at the front! Some people were known to 'fall under the power' for three days. On 'coming round' they would tell of marvellous revelations of Jesus and heaven. Some people today are concerned if anyone 'falls under the power', laughs in the Spirit, or gets delivered from demons. But we haven't even experienced what the early Salvationists experienced yet! We need the power of the Holy Spirit in our lives and ministries if we are ever going to reach this world for Jesus. It is He who convicts the world of guilt in regard to sin, righteousness and judgement (John 16:8); it is He who causes miraculous healings and demonstrations of power in and through the Body of Christ (Acts 1:8; 1 Corinthians 2:4; Hebrews 2:4). Jesus Himself did no miracles until after His baptism at Jordan when He was *'filled with the Holy Spirit'* (Luke 4:1). He had laid aside His heavenly glory and privileges (Philippians 2:7), and therefore ministered *as a man* under the anointing of the Holy Spirit (Acts 10:38). And following the resurrection, Jesus wouldn't even allow His own apostles who had trained under Him for three years, to testify of His resurrection until they had received *'power from on high'* (Luke 24:49). If He needed the power of the Spirit, and the apostles needed it, then so do we!

## A Pentecostal/Charismatic doctrine?

It has become popular, in some parts of the Western Church, to believe that you can have the gifts of the Spirit without the 'Pentecostal' experience of the 'baptism in the Holy Spirit'. While undoubtedly such a position has opened up some parts of the Church to the Holy Spirit in a way that they might not have been before (having been opposed to the teaching in some parts of the Pentecostal movement that tongues is the initial evidence of infilling), it has actually left the Church weaker in terms of learning how to stay full of the Holy Spirit personally, and thus being able to stand on one's own two feet in God. Any believer who is 'open' to the Spirit of God can 'catch the wave' of a particular 'move of God', but what happens when that particular 'move' is over (there are 'seasons' in God, 'times of refreshing' and 'restoration', cf. Acts 3:19–21)? Are they still moving in the power of the Holy Spirit? We must learn to be filled, and stay filled with the Spirit of God. The teaching of the baptism in the Holy Spirit is not a 'Pentecostal doctrine'. Far from it! It is a biblical doctrine, and a vital New Testament experience available for *every believer* today. May it never be that like the five foolish virgins in Matthew 25:1–13, when the Bridegroom comes, we will find ourselves in a place where we have to be saying to our fellow believers, 'Please, give me some of your oil, my lamp is going out!' (oil, in Scripture, is often used to portray the anointing of the Spirit). The light of Christ in our lives is fuelled by an intimate, personal relationship with Jesus in the power of the Holy Spirit. In John 7:37–39 Jesus lifted His voice and said,

' "*If anyone thirsts, let him come* [Greek: and keep coming] *to Me and drink* [Greek: and keep drinking]. *He who believes in Me, as the Scripture has said, out of his heart will flow* [Greek: keep flowing], **rivers** *of living water!" But this He spoke concerning the Spirit . . .* '

While it is true that we can receive impartation of the Spirit through the laying on of hands from fellow believers, or through the spoken word, etc., it is vitally important that we learn how to receive and walk in the power of the Holy Spirit on an ongoing basis for ourselves.

## The work of the Spirit

Since we are biblically commanded to *'be filled with the Spirit'* (see Ephesians 5:18–21), we need to know what the Holy Spirit actually does. As part of the Godhead, He was involved in creation (Genesis 1:2). As once He brooded over the formless earth, so now He broods over nations, communities, churches and individuals. But He does nothing until the word is spoken, either from God's mouth, or from ours! Yes, this is a partnership. We are *'God's fellow workers'* (1 Corinthians 3:9). When the word is spoken in faith, the Spirit works to make it happen! It is He who inspired the writing of the Holy Scriptures (2 Peter 1:20–21), who anointed prophets, priests and kings (and judges before them), and indeed all those great heroes of faith we read about in Hebrews 11. Every prophetic utterance, every miraculous healing and every supernatural demonstration of God's power was the work of the Holy Spirit, and it's that self-same Holy Spirit who lives in you and me! Every time you open your Bible and read of a miracle, say to yourself, 'That's the work of the Greater One, who lives in me!' (see 1 John 4:4). He's the same Spirit who raised Christ Jesus from the dead (Romans 8:11). The Church, as a whole (at least in the Western world), has not yet fully realised the incredible power that is available to us. Now and again (and thank God there is a great move of God all over the world today – for those who would walk in it) men and women of God have risen up in faith and moved in something of a greater dimension.

John G. Lake, at the turn of the twentieth century in South Africa, records how deadly diseases, such as the bubonic plague, would die on contact with his hand, much to the astonishment of the medical professionals seeking to effect a cure. Indeed, in recent years, the reports of miraculous healings, and the dead being raised proliferate. I asked sixty leaders in Rwanda how many of them had seen the dead raised (I was very specific: only those who had been dead for at least two days!). Twenty of them said they had. In China, it is reported as a common occurrence. It is the Spirit of God who enables such miraculous demonstrations of God's power, and it is this Holy Spirit who lives in you and me! When we cease to relate to miracles as 'unusual' and start to relate to them as a 'wondrous normality', praying, preaching and ministering in agreement with heaven, we will see much greater demonstrations of His power.

Let's consider some of the Holy Spirit's works:

1. The Holy Spirit empowers us to be a witness for Jesus, in boldness and demonstration (Acts 1:8; 4:31; 1 Corinthians 12:1–11).

2. The Holy Spirit is our Helper, Comforter, Counsellor, Strengthener and Standby (John 14:16). He comes alongside us to help us in our praying (notice He won't do it for us, but He will help *us*), interceding for us according to the perfect will of God (Romans 8:26–27).

3. He is the Spirit of truth, the Teacher who will guide us into all truth (John 14:17, 26; 16:13). We can trust Him to lead and guide us, always in line with His written Word, and always in His peace (Colossians 3:15).

4. He will bring to your remembrance what Jesus has said (John 14:26; Acts 11:15–16).

5. He has a unique relationship with the Church to testify of Jesus to the world (John 15:26–27; Revelation 22:17). You never witness alone!

6. He is the Spirit of adoption, by whom we cry out 'Abba, Father'. He bears witness with our spirit that we are children of God (Romans 8:15–16).

7. He convicts the world of sin, righteousness and judgement (John 16:8).

8. He speaks what He hears from Jesus to the Church, individually and corporately (John 16:13).

9. He will tell us the things that are to come (John 16:13).

10. He will glorify Jesus (John 16:14).

11. He will develop Christ-like character in us as we walk with Him and behold the Lord in our worship, prayer and meditation in the Word (Galatians 5:22; 1 Corinthians 3:18).

12. He will impart spiritual gifts to encourage, exhort, and build up the Body of Christ (1 Corinthians 12:1–11).

13. He will fill us with 'might' in our inner beings, our spirit, providing us with strength, stability and power for ministry (Ephesians 3:16).

14. He will give us dreams and visions (Acts 2:17).

No wonder Jesus said,

> *'It is to your advantage that I go away; for if I do not go away, the Helper will not come to you; but if I depart, I will send Him to you.'* (John 16:7)

Because Jesus went to the Father, we can do the works that He did and even greater wonders (John 14:12). This is because the Spirit by whom Jesus did miracles (Acts 10:38; Luke 4:18–19), who was given after Jesus was glorified (John 7:39; Acts 2:1–4), now indwells us, empowering us to do His works today. That which He began to do and teach before His death and resurrection, He continues to do and teach through His Church (Matthew 28:18–20; Acts 1:1). To reveal Jesus fully to the world, we need both His character and His power. This is provided for us in both the fruit (Galatians 5:22) and gifts of the Spirit (1 Corinthians 12:1–11). We need both. The Holy Spirit, through the apostle Paul, commands,

> *'Pursue love, and desire spiritual gifts, but especially that you might prophesy.'* (1 Corinthians 14:1)

Both are required! Love by itself is not sufficient, it must have supernatural expression.

## Didn't I get it all at salvation?

In response to this question, the late Dr Martin Lloyd-Jones remarked, 'Some people say they got it all at salvation. Got it all at salvation? Well, if you got it all at salvation, in the name of God, where is it?'

A friend and fellow minister in the Philippine Islands shared with me how the Lord had filled him with the Holy Spirit. He had been radically saved out of a militant organisation associated with terrorist activities, and had strongly felt the call of God upon his life to go and preach the gospel around the mostly Muslim-populated islands of Mindanoa. He began to seek God for His power to accomplish the work that he felt He was calling him to, and after several days of prayer in his hut, he heard the noise of the locals outside shouting, 'Fire, fire!' and throwing water at the roof. There was no physical fire, but the Holy Spirit had mani-fested Himself as on the Day of Pentecost, and Bonifacio was baptised in the Holy Spirit from that day onwards. At last count, he had pioneered nearly one hundred churches in Mindanoa.

In John 4:14, in the context of talking to the woman at the well, Jesus says,

> '... whoever drinks of the water that I shall give him will never thirst. But the water that I shall give him will become in him a **fountain** of water, springing up into **everlasting life**.'

The subject matter is clear: eternal life (the Greek word *zoe* means 'life as God has it'). But in John 7:37–39, Jesus promises His followers *'rivers of living water'*, which John explains with great clarity: *'this He spoke **concerning the Spirit**'*. Following the resurrection, Jesus appears to the disciples, breathes on them and says, *'Receive the Holy Spirit'* (John 20:22), but Luke also records that Jesus still tells them to *'tarry in the city of Jerusalem until you are endued with power from on high'* (Luke 24:49). Jesus, as the last Adam and the First Man of the New Creation of God, became a *life-giving spirit*. Just as God created the first Adam by forming him from the dust and breathing on him, Jesus began the New Creation of God by breathing on these vessels of clay (the disciples), and imparting to them the very life of God. They were born again. Yet not until Acts 2:1–4 were they baptised in the Holy Spirit, and thus equipped to proclaim the resurrected Christ by the power of the very One who raised Him from the dead (Romans 1:4; 8:11). What is of further interest still, is that Paul the apostle, who wrote over a third of the New Testament and had visions of incredible glory about which he was forbidden to speak (2 Corinthians 12:4), inquired of some Ephesian believers, *'Did you receive the Holy Spirit when you believed?'* (Acts 19:2). To ask such a question demands logically that it must be possible for someone who believes *not* to receive the Spirit. In fact, following the move of God that broke out under Philip's ministry in Samaria (Acts 8:4–13), the apostles in Jerusalem (who trained under Jesus!),

> *'... sent Peter and John to them, who, when they had come down, prayed for them that they might receive the Holy Spirit. For as yet He had fallen upon none of them.* **They had only been baptized in the name of the Lord Jesus.'** (Acts 8:14–16)

Clearly, the baptism in the Holy Spirit *is* an experience separate from salvation.

## What about tongues?

Much has been said to 'down-play' the importance of speaking in other tongues in recent years, but it remains a vital part of the believer's walk in the Spirit if he/she is indeed to live a life full of the Holy Spirit. Some have said that it is the 'least' of the gifts since tongues and their interpretation are last in the list of gifts mentioned in 1 Corinthians 12:1–11. However, applying the same logic, self-control would then have to be the least of the fruit of the Spirit since it comes at the end of the list in Galatians 5:22–23, and love would have to be the least of those qualities which eternally endure, since there remains faith, hope and ... love (1 Corinthians 13:13). Such arguments simply don't hold up to honest biblical exegesis. What is intriguing is that in Acts

10–11, where we have the account of Peter preaching the gospel for the first time in a Gentile's home (Cornelius), the importance of speaking in other tongues to the New Testament Church is unmistakably clear. While Peter was still explaining the gospel to them, the Holy Spirit fell upon them, and they all began to speak with other tongues and to magnify God! The Jewish believers were astounded that the Holy Spirit had been poured out on the Gentiles in exactly the same way as He had been poured out on them. How did they know it was the Holy Spirit? Acts 10:46 says, *'For they heard them speak with tongues and magnify God.'* What is more, Peter, without taking them through any prayer or confession of repentance and faith, orders them to be baptised, saying,

> *'Can anyone forbid water, that these should not be baptized who have received the Holy Spirit just as we have?'*       (Acts 10:47)

On returning to Jerusalem, Peter finds himself having to explain his conduct to the Jewish brothers there and, repeating the story, he ends up by saying,

> *'If therefore God gave them the same gift as He gave us when we believed on the Lord Jesus Christ, who was I that I could withstand God?'*       (Acts 11:17)

Their response?

> *' . . . they became silent; and they glorified God, saying, "Then God has also granted to the Gentiles repentance to life." '*
> (Acts 11:18)

In the final analysis, what was it that persuaded them that God had granted salvation to the rest of the world (a fairly major theological decision to make, to say the least!)? Undeniably, there were contributory factors such as the angelic visitation, the vision of the blanket descending from heaven, the fact that the Spirit so clearly led Peter and reminded him of Jesus' words, but nevertheless, according to Acts 10:44–47, the major factor was simply that they heard them speak with tongues and magnify God. Jesus Himself said, *'these signs shall follow those that believe. In My name they will . . . speak with new tongues'* (Mark 16:17).

## New Testament patterns of receiving the Holy Spirit

In the book of Acts there are four different accounts of people being 'baptised in the Holy Spirit'. In three of the four it directly says, 'they spoke with other tongues' (2:4; 10:46; 19:6), and in the fourth it is inferred that something physical and tangible occurred because Simon the sorcerer, *seeing* that the Holy Spirit was given by the laying on of the apostles' hands, offered them money saying,

> *'Give me this power also, that anyone on whom I lay hands may receive the Holy Spirit.'* (Acts 8:19)

In Acts 2:4 it says,

> *'And they were all filled with the Holy Spirit, and began to speak with other tongues, as the Spirit gave them utterance.'*

Note that *they* spoke. The Holy Spirit gave them the words, but *they* did the speaking. The Holy Spirit never takes over a person's will. As the apostle Paul said in 1 Corinthians 14:15, *'I **will** pray with the spirit'*. It is we who do the speaking, and, if we are believers, we can be sure that the Spirit we receive will be from God, for Jesus said,

> *'If a son asks for bread from any father among you, will he give him a stone? Or if he asks for a fish, will he give him a serpent instead of a fish? Or if he asks for an egg, will he offer him a scorpion? If you then, being evil, know how to give good gifts to your children, how much more will your heavenly Father give the Holy Spirit to those who ask Him!'* (Luke 11:11–13)

Basically, what you ask for is what you get!

Notice that in Acts 2, the first time the Jews received the Holy Spirit, *everyone* in that upper room started speaking in other tongues and, in Acts 10, the first time the Gentiles received the Holy Spirit, *everyone* spoke with other tongues. In Acts 19, after having heard that the Ephesian believers didn't even know there was a Holy Spirit, Paul was greatly surprised and asked, *'Into what then were you baptized?'* It is clear that the New Testament understanding was that when new converts were baptised in water, they should also receive the baptism in the Holy Spirit (cf. Acts 2:38). On hearing that they had only been baptised into John's baptism, he took them and re-baptised them, this time into the name of Jesus,

> *'And when Paul had laid hands on them, the Holy Spirit came upon them and they spoke with tongues and prophesied.'*
>
> (Acts 19:6)

## Seven benefits of speaking in other tongues

1.  It is an evidence of the baptism in the Holy Spirit, and an ongoing reminder of His indwelling presence (Acts 2:4).

2.  It aids intercession (Romans 8:26–27). When we don't know what to pray for as we ought, the Holy Spirit intercedes for us with groanings too deep for words (some translators: 'for intelligible speech'). While they certainly include tongues, the groanings of the Spirit are not limited to this particular expression.

3.  It is a sign for unbelievers (1 Corinthians 14:22) and aids evangelism. Many times, both in this nation and overseas, God has given believers the language of the nation/people group in which they are called to serve Him at that time, and sometimes the understanding of it too. I remember praying for a young man in Chile who didn't know a word of English, but when I prayed for him to be baptised in the Spirit, he started declaring the praises of God in perfect English. When he stopped speaking in tongues, he reverted to Latin American Spanish and was totally unable to speak a word of English!

4.  It edifies the believer. Paul says, *'he who speaks in a tongue edifies himself'* (1 Corinthians 14:4). The word 'edifies' has a variety of meanings in New Testament Greek, and could be translated 'charges himself', 'improves himself', 'builds himself up'.

5.  It gives the believer the ability to give thanks well (1 Corinthians 14:16–17).

6.   It builds faith (Jude 20)

7.   It brings rest and refreshing (Isaiah 28:11–12).

There are a number of other benefits that can certainly be inferred from Scripture, and that I have personally experienced: for example, receiving the mind of the Spirit for situations, or revelation concerning the Word (1 Corinthians 2:9–12), and the bringing of the tongue into subjection to the Lordship of Jesus (James 3:2–8, no man can tame the tongue, but the Holy Spirit can!) and, through that, the whole body! It is interesting to note that John G. Lake, whom I mentioned earlier with regard to his great experiences of the power of God, noted in his memoirs that everything he had in his ministry under God he owed to the simple gift of speaking with other tongues. There is much more to this simple gift than many would dare to say.

## How do I receive the Holy Spirit?

The Holy Spirit is a *gift*. You cannot earn Him: you must simply receive Him. Jesus said that the world cannot receive the Spirit of truth. Therefore the first condition is that you must be born again. Come to Jesus, the Lamb of God who takes away the sin of the world. Believe He died for you and rose again, and confess Him as Lord. You shall be saved (Romans 10:9–10). He is also the baptiser in the Holy Spirit (John 1:29–34). He may bring to mind specific sins you need to confess, or people you need to forgive. Spend some moments now doing just that and renouncing those past sins, if you have not already done so, especially any involvement with the occult. Believe that He cleanses and sets you free (1 John 1:9).

Now ask the Lord to fill you with His Spirit and, according to His Word, believe you receive at that very moment you ask (Mark 11:24). As you start to thank Him in faith, open your mouth and begin to speak whatever He gives you, believing that it will be the Holy Spirit (Luke 11:13). Take time to receive and drink deeply of His Spirit. Words will start to flow from within you: prayers and praises in a heavenly language – keep speaking and more will come. Jesus promised 'rivers', not a 'trickle'. There are many languages in the Holy Spirit, in fact, the Bible calls this gift *'the tongues of men and of angels'* (1 Corinthians 13:1). The more you speak in tongues, the more you will be edified, thankful, full of faith, sensitive to the Spirit's leadings, empowered for ministry and refreshed in God.

I was once at a leadership conference sitting next to a Ghanaian pastor as we listened to the preacher exhort us in the need for the power of the Spirit in our lives and ministries. At the end of that session, my Ghanaian friend, who was already overseeing four churches and much involved in evangelistic work in the rural parts of Ghana, turned to me and said, 'Jon, I have been waiting on God for four years for this gift, and I still don't speak in tongues!' He was clearly very thirsty for God, but had sadly been wrongly taught as far as receiving the Holy Spirit was concerned. I asked him why he had waited so long, to which he replied, 'Luke 24:49 says, "tarry".' I answered, 'Brother, it says, "tarry in the city of Jerusalem until you are endued with power from on high"! If you were going to take that literally for now, you would at least have to go and wait in Jerusalem, just to be scriptural!' Seeing that I was being light-hearted with him, he smiled and relaxed. Then I added, 'But can you remember one time in the book of Acts after Pentecost when people wanting to receive the Holy Spirit were sent back to Jerusalem to wait there until they were filled?' He answered, 'No!' The truth began to 'dawn on him' that the Holy Spirit is here, now, as close to us as the air we breathe, and we just have to receive Him. He stopped 'tarrying' that moment, got down on his knees and received the baptism in the Holy Spirit, praying in tongues for four hours. He has since gone on to know a new power in his ministry and planted more churches for the glory of God! Don't wait to receive. Jesus, the Baptiser in the Holy Spirit, is waiting for you right now and He will fill you the moment you ask!

Let's pray:

Father, I thank You for giving me the gift of Your Son, Jesus. I believe He died for me and rose again from the dead to give me a new life. I turn from all my sins, and I put my faith in You. Lord Jesus, I come to You, not only as my Lord and

Saviour, but as the Baptiser in the Holy Spirit. Fill me now, Lord, with Your Power, and grant me the gift of speaking in other tongues as the Spirit gives me utterance. Holy Spirit, I receive You now, and by faith I now open my mouth to praise You in my new heavenly language. In Jesus' name, Amen.

Now go ahead, open your mouth and speak out in that new language. He's filling you now. It's a love gift from Your Father who is Love. Spend a few moments just thanking Him and worshipping Him in the Spirit.

## What can I expect?

Now that you are filled with the Holy Spirit, you can expect Him to manifest in your life in ways that you have never before experienced. Keep speaking in tongues, day by day. Exchange just having a set-time-of-day 'prayer life' for 'a life of prayer' (both is best: in a marriage times of greater intimacy fill the day to day with greater love and closeness – it's the same with God!). Pray in tongues before you read your Bible and you'll often find you experience a strong sense of His presence as you read, as new thoughts and revelations enter your heart, moving you to worship, intercession and confession. Expect to meet with the Living Word in the midst of the written Word.

As you continue to stay full of the Spirit, you may find yourself getting impressions, pictures/visions in your spirit (painted on the screen of your mind) or scriptures showing you how you can pray for problems you or others you know may be facing. You may be given wisdom and insight for a particular situation, telling you about things you could never know naturally – this is called 'a word of knowledge'. Such insight can even come in dreams, though more usually when you are reaching out for them in times of prayer, ministry or worship. The Holy Spirit is a person, not just an experience! Getting 'baptised in the Spirit' is just the doorway to the Spirit-filled life – a life lived out in relationship with Him. We are made in the image of God and, therefore, just as we have emotions, intellect and will, so does He.

The Holy Spirit enables us to feel when He is grieved or delighted, and causes His thoughts to rise in our hearts. When we walk right with Him we will know His peace, but when we disobey Him – when our will and His will cross – we 'lose our peace'. But then we just need to stop, turn around (repent) and start going His way again. Let that peace be the umpire in your heart, directing every decision in life (Colossians 3:15). You can have a thousand and one prophecies, but without that peace, you cannot and must not proceed. To do so can be very costly indeed!

You may find that when you step out to pray for the sick, you experience sensations in your own body that correspond to the problems the afflicted person is facing, letting you know exactly what to pray for (they disappear after you have declared or acted on them); sometimes your hands might get warm, or even hot, and only cool down after you have laid them on the sick that they might be healed. You might experience a sudden rise of faith within you that is beyond your normal level of faith. When you do, step out in response to your faith. Expect the miraculous. These expressions are just some of the ways the Holy Spirit moves in and through our lives in the gifts of the Spirit (1 Corinthians 12:1–11). It is beyond the scope of this present chapter to have a detailed look into the gifts of the Spirit, but none the less, understand that the Holy Spirit is always ready to manifest, and when we reach out to hear His voice, to release His miracles into needy lives, His Word, His Presence, His Power are there to meet us and minister through us in the name of Jesus Christ. God always moves when faith is present.

I've seen Him open the eyes of the blind and the ears of the deaf, make cripples walk, and instantly heal those with tumours or goitres. I have seen little children born deaf and dumb suddenly start to hear and speak for the first time. Sometimes I have felt great surges of power; sometimes nothing. Don't look to the feeling, look to Jesus: trust His promise, and step out by faith! If we can do something in our own ability, He has no reason to do it. The Spirit of God is living in you for a reason: to bring the saving, healing, delivering power of God to a sin-sick world. Step out in Spirit-led reckless faith today, beyond the realms of your confidence, your ability, and into His!

## Application

1. Consider Jesus' parable about the five wise and five foolish virgins (Matthew 25:1–13). Which category do you fall into? Study Ephesians 5:18–21 to discover ways in which we can continually be full of the Spirit of God.

2. Reread the section entitled 'The Work of the Spirit'. Consider how well you know the Holy Spirit and spend some time asking the Father to reveal His ways to you more clearly that you might glorify Jesus more in your life and ministry. If you have not received the Holy Spirit, return to the prayer at the bottom of the section entitled 'How do I receive the Holy Spirit?' Come to Jesus in faith and be filled with His Spirit today.

3. Take another look at the 'Seven benefits of speaking in other tongues'. How big a part has speaking in tongues played in your life? Think about how you would like to grow in this gift.

# Chapter 5

# The Covenant Maker

In *The Chambers Dictionary* the word 'militant' is defined as 'engaged in warfare; actively contending; strenuously active in support of a particular cause'. As Christians we are engaged in a war for souls; we are contending for the faith of the gospel; we are strenuously active in the cause of Christ! I believe that God moves with the man or woman who moves in faith to advance the Kingdom of God in the lives of people, communities and nations – and indeed *there is* a longing in the hearts of many believers in the Western world for a great revival to sweep our nations, turning the hearts of multitudes in repentance and faith to Jesus Christ. However, if we are going to see God moving by His power to accomplish mighty miracles and reaping a great harvest of precious souls through the proclamation of the gospel, we need to understand what it is that moves the hand of God to do such works through the lives of those who believe Him.

In the Gospels we see that Jesus went about all Galilee, teaching in the synagogues, preaching the gospel of the Kingdom, and healing all kinds of sickness and disease, with the result that great multitudes followed Him (Matthew 4:23–24). We know that through the hands of the apostles many signs and wonders were done amongst the people, with the result that believers were increasingly added to the Lord, and the sick and demonised were *all* healed (Acts 5:12–16). Is it possible that they understood something about God's dealings with human beings that many of us in the West have little or no understanding of?

I have stood on platforms around the world and seen thousands come to Christ in a single meeting, with miracles abounding as people come in simple faith to Jesus, and I know that what was happening in those gatherings was no accident. There is something that people in the developing world understand that many in the so-called 'civilised world' with their secularised materialistic world view have no idea of, and sadly this is very often true of the Church also. It is not only their belief in and experience of the spirit world; it is not only their greater intensity in prayer and fasting: it is also their faith in the simple, but deeply profound truth that God has made a *covenant* with them. In this last foundational chapter, before we move on to the application of 'militant Christianity', we are going to look at one of God's most powerful 'secrets'. It is a secret that He reveals only to a particular kind of person: those who *fear* the Lord.

> *'The secret of the* Lord *is with those who fear* **him**,
> *And* **He** *will show* [reveal] *them His* **covenant**.'*
> (Psalm 25:14)

May I impress upon you the need to come before God with this truth in an attitude of genuine reverence and respect, for it stands right at the centre of God's ways and dealings with mankind and, if properly understood, embraced and applied will quite literally change your life and ministry forever.

## The nature of covenant

Covenant is a concept that goes right through the Bible from beginning to end. In fact, ever since the Fall, in all God's dealings with human beings, a covenant has had to be in place. Furthermore, all these covenants are sealed in blood for the blood is the price for our sin – a life for a life – the provision of God for us, satisfying His justice against sin, and therefore enabling Him to extend His mercy towards us (Leviticus 17:11). It is a concept seen right from the beginning in Genesis 3:21, when God sacrificed an animal and covered Adam and Eve with its skins, prefiguring Christ's sacrifice for us clothing us with His righteousness, right through to the New Covenant, established on better promises (Hebrews 7:22), sealed in the blood of Jesus Christ that we enjoy today. Following the flood, we see Noah offering a sacrifice, in response to which God made a covenant with mankind never to flood the earth again. Then we have the Abrahamic covenant, where God credits or imputes righteousness to Abraham by grace on the basis of faith and faith alone, which is the Old Testament model of our covenant with God in the New Testament (or 'Covenant'). And, of course, there is the Mosaic covenant, with its laws, blessings and curses that God made with the people of Israel. Yet this concept of covenant goes so deep in the heart and plan of God that, even before creation, Jesus was *'the Lamb slain from before the foundation of the world'* (Revelation 13:8). God was not 'caught out' by the fall of the human race: He had a great rescue plan already in place, a plan to redeem us ('buy us back' from sin and its consequences), and restore us to a place of eternal relationship with Him, and all the blessings that such a relationship entails. It should be a source of great comfort and rejoicing to know that before sin, there was salvation; before sickness, there was healing; before death, there was life – and that life is ours in Jesus Christ. As one great preacher once commented, 'Everything God has foreseen, He has seen-for!'

In every use of the word 'covenant' there is the understanding that something 'binding' and permanent is being dealt with. Both the Hebrew word *berit* and the Greek word *diatheke* carry this sense of a binding, permanent contract, a will or agreement between two parties, necessitating certain obligations, and resulting in certain benefits. As we turn to Genesis 15:1–18, to consider the nature of the covenant we have with God, as typified in His dealings with Abraham, we will see that there are basically four aspects to the outworking of His covenant in our lives. These four aspects can be summarised as:

1. promise(s)

2. faith

3. sacrifice

4. responsibility.

## Promise(s)

In Genesis 15 we read the account of how the Lord came to Abram in a vision, and promised him four things: firstly, that God Himself would be his *'shield'* (protection); secondly that God would be his *'exceedingly great reward'* (prosperity); thirdly, that he would have a child from his own body in his old age (miraculous physical restoration, particularly since this promise covered Sarah too!); and, lastly, that he would be succeeded by a multitude of descendants (posterity, increase and influence). It is God who initiated this covenant with Abraham, and God who has initiated covenant with us. John 15:16 declares,

> *'You did not choose Me, but **I chose you** and appointed you that you should go and bear fruit, and that your fruit should remain, that **whatever** you ask the Father in My name, He may give you.'*

God made a covenant with us not to destroy us, but to save us, not to impoverish us, but to prosper us, not to make us sick, but to restore us to fullness of life, fullness of health, enabling us to fulfil His destiny on our lives, that we might be a blessing to the nations and to the generations yet to come! He is the God who keeps covenant (Daniel 9:4) and promises,

> *'My covenant I will **not** break,*
> *Nor alter the word that has gone out of My lips.'*  (Psalm 89:34)

## Faith

The natural result of receiving a promise (or promises) from God is faith (Romans 10:17). Abraham *'believed in the* Lord, *and He accounted it to him for righteousness'* (Genesis 15:6). That word 'accounted' in the Hebrew literally means that God calculated all that it meant for Abraham to believe Him, and concluded that that was equal to righteousness. Righteousness is the state of being and doing right before God. This meant that regardless of Abraham's past, regardless of his failings, because he believed the promises God made to him, God would treat him as though every thought, word or deed that Abraham had ever had, spoken or done, yes, even his very being, was righteous in His sight. Romans 4:23–25 tells us,

> *'Now it was not written for his sake alone that it* [righteousness] *was imputed to him, but **also for us**. It shall be imputed to us who believe in Him who raised up Jesus our Lord from the dead, who was delivered up because of our offences, and was raised because of our justification.'*

This righteousness means that we are now accepted by God, in agreement and partnership with Him, and there is nothing standing between us that can separate us from Him, nor from the fulfilment of His promises in our lives. Faith does not look at the obstacles in the way, it only looks at Jesus, believing His word. It is the substance of things hoped for, the evidence of things *not* seen (*'faith perceiving as **real fact** what is not revealed to the senses'*, Hebrews 11:1 Amplified Bible). It chooses to think, talk and act as if the things that God has spoken are already so (Romans 4:16–21), regardless of the feelings, circumstances or opposition that would suggest to the contrary. Thus persevering, faith obtains the promise, releasing on the earth what God has already done in the heavenlies.

## Sacrifice

Now we come to the real issue, the very principle that releases the miracle-working, life-changing power of God in and through our lives. Without it, we are *'strangers from the covenants of promise, having no hope and without God in the world'* (Ephesians 2:12).

Abraham experienced God in a way that most of us long for. God came to him in a vision. We can presume, since people could not yet be 'born again' and therefore have the Spirit of God 'in' them, that this was not an 'internal vision', but an 'external' one. He likely heard God speak to him in what would have been *to him* an audible voice. God physically transported him from one place to another (Genesis 15:5: *'He brought him outside'*), or at least walked with him to that location! Having already made several great promises to Abraham (Abram at this stage), He made even more, promising him and his descendants the land in which he dwelt. In the midst of such dramatic supernatural manifestation of God's presence and glory, Abram had the seeming audacity to ask, *'how shall I know that I will inherit it?'* (v. 8). For most of us, God's physical presence, audible voice, and wonderful promises (that always produce faith in the heart anyway: Romans 10:17) would have been enough. But not for Abram. He was an Eastern man and knew that until blood had been shed in the making of a solemn covenant, there was nothing *final* or *certain* about it.

God told Abram to bring a three-year-old heifer, a three-year-old female goat, a three-year-old ram, a turtledove, and a young pigeon. All except the birds were cut in two. Blood was shed, covenant was being made. Hebrews 6:13–18 tells us,

> *'For when God made a promise to Abraham, because He could swear by no one greater, He swore by **Himself**, saying, "Surely blessing I will bless you, and multiplying I will multiply you." And so, after he had patiently endured, he obtained the promise. For men indeed swear by the greater, and an oath for confirmation is for them **an end of all dispute**. Thus God, determining to show more abundantly to the heirs of promise* [that's you and me!] *the immutability* [unchangeableness] *of His counsel* [His Word or promise], *confirmed it by an oath, that **by two unchangeable things*** [His nature and His covenant], *in which **it is impossible for God to lie** we might have strong consolation . . . '*

God, who cannot lie, has bound Himself to His own word, and His very righteousness and integrity stands behind the covenant that He has made. Furthermore, the covenant that He made with Abram was not a covenant based on human performance, but on the abounding grace of God! Genesis 15:17–18 tells us,

> *'And it came to pass, when the sun was going down and it was dark, that behold there appeared a **smoking oven** and **a burning torch** that passed between those pieces. On the same day, the* LORD *made covenant with Abram . . . '*

It was normal for both parties to pass through the pieces, declaring their loyalty to the other and to the terms of the covenant. There was an exchange of resources and identity for now each one lived for the other and the resources of both were equally theirs. Blessings for obedience to the covenant, and curses for disobedience were the normal practice of the day. However, here there is no curse, but only blessings. Not only does God initiate the covenant, He is the only One who passes between the pieces (symbolically in the 'smoking oven' and 'burning torch'), humbling Himself, even as Jesus humbled Himself, dying on the cross to make covenant with those lost in sin (in order to redeem them!). God's oath was unilateral and unconditional, with no requirements demanded of Abram. He just believed.

The implications of this awesome truth are staggering. The Abrahamic covenant was established years before the Mosaic covenant ever came into being. The Law was a schoolmaster to bring us to Christ (Galatians 3:24). But having been justified by faith, we are no longer under the schoolmaster; we no longer have to concern ourselves with the question, 'Am I good enough to be healed, provided for, delivered etc.?' The price has been paid! The blessings promised to Abraham now belong to us. Galatians 3:13–14 says,

> *'Christ has redeemed us from the curse of the law, having become a curse for us (for it is written, "Cursed is anyone who hangs on a tree"), that the blessing of Abraham might come upon the Gentiles in Christ Jesus, that we might receive the promise of the Spirit **through faith**.'*

If you want to get a good understanding of just what curses we have been redeemed from, take a look at Deuteronomy 28. All the blessings are ours by grace through faith and, through the sacrifice of Jesus upon the cross, we have been redeemed from *every* curse! Sickness and disease of every nature, confusion, poverty, defeat, breakdown: it's all there. Since we believe in Christ, the promises made to Him (as the seed of Abraham) have been made to us *in him*. We are Abraham's seed, and heirs according to the promise (Galatians 3:29 and 3:16–18).

## Responsibility

We have seen that in this mighty covenant with God, there is promise, faith and sacrifice. We rejoice that all the blessings of God have been freely given to us in Christ, and that all His promises to us are *'yes'* in Christ Jesus (2 Corinthians 1:20). But what is our part? Abraham is called *'the father of all those who believe'*, of those who *'walk in the steps of the faith which our father Abraham had'* (Romans 4:11, 12). Like Abraham, we must be willing to leave our past behind and follow the call of God, even when we don't know where we are going (Hebrews 11:8). We must be willing to sacrifice even the things we love most, and on which we place our hopes for the future, believing that God alone is our source, and He will provide (Genesis 22). We must be willing to stand in faith, in the face of contrary natural evidence, and believe God. In fact, we must learn to confront the enemy when he seeks to rob us of the blessings the sacrifice of Christ has made available for us! In Genesis 15:11, the Scripture tells us that 'vultures' (the 'birds of the air' often typify demonic forces in Scripture – see Mark 4:4, 15) came down upon the sacrifice, and it was *Abram*, not God, who *'drove them away'*. In much the same way, we must *'submit to God'*, we must *'resist the devil'*, and *'he will flee'* from us (James 4:7) We must take *'every thought into captivity to the obedience of Christ'* (2 Corinthians 10:5), and use His Word on our lips to rebuke the enemy, *'It is written . . . '* (Matthew 4:4). If symptoms attack your body, learn to resist them with His Word, declaring, 'By His stripes, I am healed!' (1 Peter 2:24). If there's no money in the bank, and the bills are coming in, declare with thanksgiving, 'My God shall supply *all* my needs according to *His* riches in glory by Christ Jesus!' (Philippians 4:19). Maintaining a 'covenant confession' releases the covenant blessings of God in your life! Romans 10:9–10 covers not only salvation, but all the benefits included in it: the Greek word translated 'salvation', *sozo*, includes the sense of being 'healed, delivered, made whole, protected'. As in all His gracious provision to us, God has given us all things that pertain to life and godliness, but we must appropriate them, imitating those who through faith and patience inherit the promises. Without such responsibility there can be no dignity, no authority, and no accountability to the God who deeply desires to reward His children both in this life, and on that great Day! God has given us the awesome privilege and responsibility of being His 'under-rulers', kings and priests unto our God. Let us embrace our new identity in Christ, standing firm on this mighty covenant of grace, and begin to reign as kings in this life (Romans 5:17).

## Releasing the blessings of Abraham

Jesus healed the sick, not only as an expression of His compassion, but also in response to faith released in His person and His promises. He is the full revelation of God (Hebrews 11:2–3; Colossians 1:15–20), the Word made flesh (John 1:14). He never turned one person away who needed healing, and *every one* who touched Him in faith was healed. What He did then, He does now. The same things that moved Him to heal and deliver then, move Him to do the same now. He is the same, yesterday, *today*, and forever (Hebrews 13:8).

In Luke 13:10–17 is recorded the account of Jesus' healing of a woman who was 'bent double' on the Sabbath day. The leader of the synagogue was furious, esteeming his religious 'dos and don'ts' more than the needs of the people, and indeed the healing power and compassion of God. But Jesus said,

> *'So, ought not this woman, being a **daughter of Abraham**, whom Satan has bound – think of it – for eighteen years, be loosed from this bond on the Sabbath?'*　　　　　(Luke 13:16)

Since we know from John 5:19 that Jesus only did the things that He saw His Father doing, we can be certain that just as it was then, so it is today: the sons and daughters of faith – of Abraham – should be loosed from the bondages of sickness that Satan has put on them! Jesus healed to fulfil the Covenant! In Matthew 8:16–17 Jesus healed them all,

> *'... that it might be fulfilled which was spoken by Isaiah the prophet, saying:*
> *"He Himself took our infirmities*
> *And bore our sicknesses." '*

He still heals to fulfil His Word (Mark 16:20). This means that to be healed, or even to minister healing, we don't need to wait until we have a specific word from God (a 'rhema'), we just need to step out by faith and boldly take/release what is ours through the 'finished work' of Jesus upon the cross.

In some circles of the Church there has been a divided message that has gone into the Body of Christ that has done much damage to the release of faith and therefore the experience of the miraculous in many lives and ministries. While acknowledging that God heals (if He can create a universe with just 'words', then surely He can heal!), the argument of some is that healing is not in the atonement (something we will shortly show to be erroneous), and therefore is a gift released through the power of the Holy Spirit, as and when God chooses to heal. This is seen as being *'the powers of the age to come'* (Hebrews 6:5), breaking through on the present age, and stems from a basic understanding of the Kingdom of God. Without going into too much deep theology on this, simply stated, if healing is not in the covenant (atonement), then it cannot be in the Kingdom! Everything we receive from God comes to us through the blood sacrifice of Jesus! Everything! Right from the very basics of salvation, forgiveness, peace in our hearts, etc., all the way through to the powerful outpouring and demonstrations of the Holy Spirit. Translated literally Isaiah 53:3–5 reads, 'He is despised and rejected by men, a man of pains and acquainted with sickness ... Surely He has borne our sicknesses and carried our pains ... He was wounded for our transgressions, He was bruised for our iniquities; the chastisement for our peace was upon Him, and by His stripes we are healed.' When was He acquainted with sickness, bearing our sicknesses and carrying our pains? It was at the same time when He was wounded for our transgressions and bruised for our iniquities! At the cross, where Jesus paid for it all.

## Same provision, different outworkings

God is sovereign, and in His sovereignty He has chosen the way that He will work, and that way is the way of Covenant. There are instant miracles (normally gifts of the Spirit, given as the Spirit wills – but if you step out in faith, you will often get such manifestations), and there are recoveries (Mark 16:17). There is healing which is instantaneous, from the outside-in (God's power and principle of life impacting and destroying sickness and the principle of death within it), and there is healing that is progressive recovery, from the inside-out (by believing the word and standing in faith with thanksgiving the healing life of God rises within you, from your spirit, into your soul, and finally fully restoring your body, i.e. Proverbs 4:20–22).

Even in Jesus' ministry we see two main approaches which are quite different. There were those who came to Jesus in faith to touch Him (either individually, or in a crowd). It was in those cases that 'everyone who touched Him was healed'. Then there were those occasions when the Spirit expressly led Jesus to one amongst many sick, and He touched/spoke to him/her (i.e., the man at the pool, John 5:2–9). In the case of the crippled man at the pool of Bethesda, the man didn't even seem to have any faith in Jesus (v. 7), but still he was healed. On that occasion, the normal process (Jesus commanding the sick person to do some-thing and then his/her physical act of faith releasing the super-natural miracle) was reversed, and the man was instantly healed before he even moved a finger. And knowing he was healed, he got up and walked. We must learn that Jesus heals in different ways and we must be sensitive to the Holy Spirit to minister as He leads. We can *always* lay hands on the sick and expect them to recover, because that is in our covenant, and healing belongs to all (Mark 16:17; 1 Peter 2:24), but we must also be sensitive to those promptings and words of knowledge that God gives, directing us to a particular individual or showing us an image of the condition in our minds (sometimes like an X-ray, or an impression in your mind, or a feeling in your body that corres-ponds to the condition in the body of the sufferer). When we have such direction, we need to follow it, for although there are often instant miracles when we are just laying hands on the sick by faith without any particular direction, many times when we have such clear instructions from the Lord, there will be dramatic demonstrations of His power. Jesus said that He only did what He saw the Father doing (John 5:19). However, He also said, *'My Father is **always** at His work'* (John 5:17 NIV). One of the reasons why some do not see much evidence of the miraculous in their lives and ministries is *not* that God is not working such miracles, but much rather that they are too busy with their own agenda to see what the Father is doing and thus move with Him! If they would only be looking to see what the Father is doing and adjust their ministry to His plans, and His ways, they would see the miracles of God in their midst. The miracles are already there in God's realm, but without a place of sensitive, obedient faith in the earth, they cannot be manifested. Let us learn to wait inwardly on God (even as we are stepping out in 'our' faith in the midst of active ministry) for His direction, His faith, and His anointing.

## True of healing, true of provision

What is true concerning God's mighty healing power, is also true concerning His provision in the area of our finances. I can't exhort you to reach out in faith for the power of God in healing without also encouraging you to believe God for the blessings of Abraham in your finances. Abraham was not a poor man. He was abundantly supplied. His God is our God, his covenant our covenant (Galatians 3:14, 29). Our God has revealed Himself as Jehovah-Jireh, 'God-Who-Provides'. This subject really deserves a chapter in itself but, briefly, I want to encourage you to step out of the boat by faith (Matthew 14:25–33), and trust God to provide. I've seen Him multiply money in wallets when we needed it in some remote area on the mission field, and provide everything to pay for even the most practical of needs when I had nothing! He promised that if we would seek first the King-dom of God and His righteousness, He would add all these other things to us (Matthew 6:33). Don't wait until you have the 'things', just *go* and God will provide! Provision follows commis-sion – as someone once said, 'For every God-given vision, there is God-given provision.' That's the Word, and that's faith – and it pleases God. Even if you don't have 'seed to sow' He'll provide it (2 Corinthians 9:10). Ask Him for seed to sow, and according to the measure you sow, you will certainly reap (2 Corinthians 9:6). Trust our great Father God – He will provide and He will prosper us as we walk in simple faith and humble obedience. If He takes care of the birds of the air, He will certainly take care of you (Matthew 6), and as you step out by faith in His service, be assured, God pays for what He orders!

## The time is *now*

In 2 Corinthians 6:2 we are told: *'Behold* **now** *is the day of salvation'* (remember *sozo* means 'healing, deliverance, wholeness and protection'). Our God is not the great 'I WAS', but the great 'I AM'. He is *always* ready, always speaking, and always working. The real issue is, are we ready, are we listening, and are we willing to lay down our agenda and start living for His? In John 11:40, Jesus said,

> *'Did I not say to you that if you would* **believe** *you would see the glory of God?'*

Please note that believing comes *before* seeing. Faith excites and releases the Holy Spirit to move in power. I have seen God perform creative miracles when I felt nothing, sometimes removing parts of a person's body that they received as a birth defect, sometimes adding something that was missing. There have been times when I knew that God was using my faith; times when it has been the faith of another just coming for prayer, believing for a miracle; and times when I felt sure it was neither my faith, nor theirs, but *His*! I recall a particular miracle that has to be one of the most instantaneous miracles I have ever seen. I and a partner in ministry were conducting some evangelistic crusades in Ghana, West Africa. Following the preaching of the gospel and leading people to Christ, we would pray for the sick 'en masse'. Our practice was always to have the miracles 'checked out' before we allowed those who had experienced healing to come on the platform to testify, but on this particular evening a man had somehow managed to get onto the platform with the help of his friends, without being 'checked over'. As usual, I put the microphone to his mouth, asking him what God had done for him, only to hear him say quite emphatically, 'I'm blind!' Wondering how this man had ever got onto the platform and hoping that maybe he had been healed of something else, I asked him again, 'God has not made you blind, sir, but what has He done for you this evening?' He replied again, 'I'm blind!', this time with the support of his friends behind him, saying, 'since birth'. We had just finished telling the people that Jesus was more powerful than the witch doctor, that Jesus Christ was the same yesterday, today and forever, and that He would heal the sick tonight, demonstrating that He is alive and here for them. There was no way out. Hundreds of people were watching, including the witches! In what felt like 'time standing still', I suddenly heard a voice coming over my right shoulder, saying, 'Receive your sight!' I turned to see who was there, since the voice was audible to me, but there was no one. Realising that the voice I heard was the Holy Spirit, I quickly turned to the man, and repeating those very words laid hands on his eyes. In a moment, like a flash of lightning, his eyes were opened, and he looked at me, stunned and overwhelmed with emotion. He could hardly stop touching my face and saying, 'I can't believe it! I can see, I can see!' I knew it wasn't his faith, and I can hardly say it was mine, but this I know: we serve a covenant-keeping, faithful God, who upholds all things by the word of His power. When it seems as if all is lost and your faith has come to its very end, be assured that Jesus, the Author and Finisher of your faith, will always be right with you, and His faith will never let you down!

Let's pray:

Father, I thank You so much for the strength of Your love and commitment to us that You have expressed in not only giving Your Son for us, but in making such a wonderful, powerful and eternal covenant with us so that we could stand with great boldness of faith in the face of every opposition, knowing for certain that You will honour Your Word and fulfil Your great promises to us. Thank you for the great privilege of working with You in an unending partnership of covenant grace to reach this world with Your love and prepare a Bride for Your Son. Today, by faith, I embrace my new identity in Christ, taking hold of my responsibility and authority in Your name. Lead me by Your Spirit, fill me with Your love, and use me for Your glory.

In Jesus' name, Amen.

## Application

1. Define the word 'covenant'. What are the implications of the New Covenant for our lives? What are its benefits and its obligations?

2. If we are going to walk in the steps of Abraham's faith, what does that entail?

3. Describe the two main ways that Jesus healed. How should this affect the way we approach ministry to the sick?

4. Do we need to see miracles before we have faith for them (John 11:40)? How do we obtain faith for the miraculous (Romans 10:17)?

# Chapter 6

# This Is War!

Jesus began His ministry by overcoming satanic opposition in the wilderness (Matthew 4:1–11) and, as soon as He entered the public forum, His very presence exposed and confronted demonic powers, leading to their expulsion (Mark 1:23–28). Throughout His earthly ministry it is frequently recorded that He cast out demons (Matthew 8:16–17, 28–32; 9:32–33, etc.) and commissioned and empowered His disciples to do the same (Matthew 10:1, 8). In fact, in Mark 16:17 deliverance is proclaimed by Jesus to be the first sign accompanying the ministry of true believers as they go into all the world preaching the gospel! In my own experience over the last fourteen years, whether it has been confronting and 'binding' demonic powers in a particular locality, or casting out demons from individuals, there has always been some measure of confrontation with Satan's evil domain. However, we can truly say, *'thanks be to God, who **always** leads us in triumph in Christ'* (2 Corinthians 2:14). We have faced all manner of things: witches trying to stop the work of God, evil spirits manifesting themselves at night, curses, threats, but *Jesus is Lord*, and His power and authority is far greater than every power of darkness. In fact, *'He who is in you is **greater** than he that is in the world'* (1 John 4:4).

As we consider this vital subject, let us be constantly reminded of the greatness of our God and the complete and irreversible triumph that Jesus won for us through His victorious death and resurrection. There has been so much taught in recent years on the subject of spiritual warfare, some things helpful and some things not. It cannot be stressed enough that the *only* final authority on this vital subject is the Word of God. It seems that in the Church we are commonly faced with two extremes as far as this issue is concerned: some forms of teaching come close to deifying the principalities and powers, attributing to them almost equal power to God Himself (which is both completely erroneous and likely demonically inspired in that its devilish 'fruit' is a misplaced faith in the enemy – i.e. fear and a crippling unbelief that binds the hearts of those who receive such teaching)! Others make the dangerous mistake of complete denial by treating the devil as if he was no threat to us at all. In every issue of life, it is the *truth*, received, believed and acted upon that sets people free (John 8:32). The Word of God is completely sufficient (2 Timothy 3:16–17) for all we need to know concerning God, the devil, and indeed ourselves. Furthermore, if our practice in spiritual warfare is not biblical, while we may stir up great zeal in prayer, frankly we will achieve little more than a sense of exhaustion from all our wasted breath – our authority is delegated and can therefore only operate within the boundaries God has set. If we are going to wage war against the enemy effectively in these last days, we must realise that true biblical authority does not flow from a great 'inside knowledge' of the *'depths of Satan'* (Revelation 2:24, i.e. knowing everything about the occult and how it works, etc.) but much rather from a living faith in Christ, the victory He accomplished over the powers of darkness through His death and resurrection, and a true submission to His Lordship in our lives.

## Our God is greater

Today, it is true that we face a huge array of demonic powers in our nations, expressed in (and largely due to) the wholesale acceptance of immorality, abortion, homosexuality, pornography, drug abuse, humanistic and relativistic philosophies, and rebellion against God and all God-ordained authority, which in turn inevitably leads to witchcraft (1 Samuel 15:23). Having ministered much in Africa and Asia, as well as in Western Europe and to a lesser extent the USA, I would say there is as much witchcraft in Western nations as there is in the developing world. It is just more sophisticated, hidden, or 'garbed' in modern terminology (such as 'New Age'). Whenever the true gospel is preached, with an uncompromised call to repentance toward God and faith in the Lord Jesus Christ, there will inevitably be confrontation with the powers of darkness. We must remember that it is often in those situations – in weather terms, like a cold front and a hot front meeting – that there is the greatest release of power, demonstrating the all-surpassing authority of the Kingdom of God! Many miracles and deliverances result, often leading to many coming to Christ. We must not fear the enemy, but rather remember that Satan is a created being, who has been placed *under* the authority of the Church because of our position in Christ Jesus (Ephesians 1:19–23; 2:6). Some have even been afraid to step out in faith and preach the gospel in power because they have been taught of the danger of counter-attack. But Jesus said,

> 'Behold, I give you the authority to trample on snakes and scorpions and over **all** the power of the enemy, and **nothing** shall by any means hurt you.' (Luke 10:19)

Beware that you do not allow the enemy to come against you through your own faith for a counter-attack! As we go out proclaiming His Word, and the power of His name, it is inevitable that we will find ourselves stirring up and confronting demonic powers, but if we are living in Him and take our place of authority in Christ with humility and dependency toward God, we shall always come forth victorious, bringing much praise and glory to our wonderful Lord Jesus, the King of kings and Lord of lords!

## Trained for battle

> 'For the weapons of our warfare are not carnal but mighty in God for pulling down strongholds.' (2 Corinthians 10:3–4)

> 'For we do not wrestle against flesh and blood, but against principalities, against powers, against the rulers of the darkness

*of this age, against spiritual hosts of wickedness in the heavenly places.'* (Ephesians 6:12)

If we are ever to be truly effective in reaching our generation for Christ, we must realise that our primary battle is not political, not physical, not financial or intellectual, but spiritual. It is certain that behind every one of those arenas, spiritual powers are at work, seeking to blind the minds of unbelievers to the gospel of Christ (2 Corinthians 4:4). There is a heavenly war (often referred to as 'the air war' by some Bible teachers today), and an earthly war. One is waged through intercession; the other through proclamation. One is waged in the secret place; the other in the public place. *Both* are spiritual warfare and *both* are necessary if we want to see the breakthrough God desires us to have, and reap the harvest He has appointed for us. It is Reinhard Bonnke, the great German evangelist, who says, 'Intercession without evangelism is like dynamite without a fuse!' We need the dynamite, and we need the fuse. When we have both, we can expect a spiritual explosion, with far-reaching implications for the Kingdom of God!

## Prayer warfare: why?

All the great evangelists, both of years gone by and in the present day, speak of the great need to overcome in the heavenlies through prayer before we experience significant breakthrough on the earth. Evan Roberts, mightily used of God in the Welsh revival of the last century wrote, 'In Luke, it does not say "preach, and faint not", but *"pray*, and faint not". It is not difficult to preach. But while you pray you are alone in some solitary place, fighting in a prayer battle against the powers of darkness, and you will know the secret of victory!'

It was D.L. Moody in the nineteenth century who said, 'Plead with God for men, before you plead with men for God.' There is a breakthrough that must happen in the realm of the spirit *first*. It is not that God is unwilling and we are somehow trying to convince Him into the notion of saving the lost or sending a great revival, for it is His will that *all* be saved (1 Timothy 2:4). It is simply that we are in a war with evil satanic powers in the heavenly places that we must 'bind' in prayer before we can plunder the lost souls under their control for the Kingdom of God (Matthew 12:29). Even in the Old Testament we learn the significance of such warfare in the heavenlies as far as answered prayer is concerned. Daniel had set himself to fast and pray to receive revelation from God concerning a vision he had received. After three whole weeks, an angel of God appeared to him, saying,

> '... from **the first day** that you set your heart to understand, and to humble yourself before your God, your words were heard; and I have come because of your words.' (Daniel 10:12)

In the next verse, the angel disclosed the reason why it had taken so long for the manifestation of answered prayer to come to Daniel: *'But the prince of the kingdom of Persia withstood me twenty-one days; and behold, Michael, one of the chief princes, came to help me'*. Delay is *not* denial! It is during these times of intense prayer warfare that we must learn to hold fast to the promises of God, living by faith and *not* by sight, believing the answer is on its way! This is surely what Jesus meant when He said, *'whatever you ask when you pray, believe that you **receive** them, and you **will** have them'* (Mark 11:24). We must trust our heavenly Father's integrity, believing His Word that what we ask for in prayer, in faith, is ours – and keep believing that until the manifestation comes! Your faith contributes to the victorious warfare in the heavenlies. In the New Testament, in Ephesians 4:8–10, we read of how Christ in His triumphant ascendancy to the Father led captivity captive, ascending far above *all* the heavens, that He might fill *all* things. Christ's authority is absolute in all three worlds – heaven, earth, and under the earth (Matthew 28:18–20; Philippians 2:9–11), but it is an authority that is primarily expressed through the Body of Christ upon the earth, and must be enforced through our faith expressed in prayer, proclamation and bold action to advance the Kingdom. In my own ministry, through the years I have seen the Lord perform many *instant* miracles, but we have also encountered delays, with unusual breakthroughs after a period of time in answer to continued, faith-filled prayer. On one occasion, on the small island of Chile Chico, off the coast of Chile, South America, we held a mission where, as well as many being saved, there were a number of significant healings. However, we had laid hands on many more sick people than we had seen instantly healed. But following our return to the UK, the local pastors contacted our Chilean representative to tell him that on the same day, thirteen weeks later, every person that we laid hands on was instantly and perfectly healed! There is a war in the heavenlies, and there is a need for persevering faith-filled prayer. Having done all, stand! Our God is a faithful God.

## Whose world is it?

In the beginning, God gave Adam authority over all the earth (Genesis 1:26). The psalmist declared,

> 'The heaven, even the heavens, are the LORD's;
> But the earth He has given to the children of men.'
>
> (Psalm 115:16; see also Psalm 8:6)

However, through his rebellion against the Lord, man's authority fell into the hands of the enemy, a fact that Jesus didn't dispute when Satan offered Him all the kingdoms of this world and their glory if He would only fall down and worship him (Luke 4:6). It is through Jesus, the Last Adam, that authority is restored to redeemed humanity because of His sinless life, substitutionary death and victorious resurrection. Jesus has *all* authority in heaven *and* on earth (Matthew 28:18–19). Furthermore, this authority is not a return to 'Adamic authority' but through Christ we are partakers of His authority!

However, in this dispensation of grace, God has given human beings free will to choose or reject His offer of forgiveness and eternal life. We can choose to have dominion (through Christ) or be dominated (by the devil)! Those who live in rebellion to God, remain under the dominion of Satan, the prince of the power of the air (Ephesians 2:2) and god of this world system (2 Corinthians 4:4). Those who repent and believe in Jesus, are saved and enter, through Christ, into a place of dominion by living in submission to God. The simple truth is that Satan is the god of all rebels. When people act in rebellion to God, it gives Satan place to exercise legal authority in the earth. However, when people live in submission to God, they give place for the Lordship of Christ to be powerfully manifested in the earth. On a number of occasions, when pioneering in the gospel, I have been personally confronted with demonic powers, openly manifesting themselves and seeking to prevent the work of God in that area from succeeding, and every time when that spirit was bound in the name of Jesus, there was great breakthrough leading to many being saved, healed and delivered. On one occasion we were in Slovakia, preaching in an area where there were apparent 'apparitions' of 'Mary' speaking to children, in particular, and telling them all manner of things that were frankly nothing more than total deception (they did not glorify Jesus, nor were they biblical). In the afternoon, I felt led by the Spirit of God to come against this 'deceiving spirit' in prayer, commanding it to stop manifesting, release the people from its grip (thousands gathered every month to hear the so-called 'revelations') and leave. To my surprise, in the middle of prayer, I was suddenly confronted by a manifestation (so real it was almost visible to the physical eye) of this spirit's face in my bedroom, looking like 'Mary' and asking me why I was coming against it, imploring me to leave it alone and suggesting that it was doing no harm to the people! I could feel the manipulative, drawing power of this spirit trying to seduce me to accept its words and become more tolerant and accepting of its rule over these people. However, I spoke to it firmly, telling it that it was *not* 'Mary' but rather the false 'queen of heaven' that is often worshipped in such nations, and commanding it to leave in the name of Jesus. Remarkably, the face of 'Mary' was suddenly removed, as if a mask had been peeled off, to reveal a grotesque beast that roared at me and disappeared! There was a tremendous sense of spiritual breakthrough and that night nearly everyone in the building (approximately 200 people, in a fairly remote country village) gave their lives to Christ and there were many healed and delivered from evil spirits. Three children who had been born deaf and dumb, all started hearing and speaking for the first time in their lives –

praise God! Accounts of this kind of encounter could be repeated many times over, not only from our own ministry but from many preachers of the gospel around the world. The simple truth is that the enemy dominates lives, families and communities to the level of our *tolerance* of him! But when we arise as the Church of Jesus Christ, taking our authority in the name of Jesus, we will see him flee in terror, and many saved for the glory of God.

## Bind and plunder!

Since the devil has been stripped of his authority through Christ (Colossians 2:15), his main power operates in the areas of deception, lies and the seduction of human beings, causing them to live in a place of spiritual blindness without Christ (2 Corinthians 4:4). It is the privilege and responsibility of the Church to exercise her God-given authority (Ephesians 3:10) to make known to the principalities and powers in the heavenly places the manifest wisdom of God (i.e. Christ – 1 Corinthians 1:30), binding them in Jesus' name and by the power of His Word. Christ has already overcome the enemy so that we may exercise authority in the realm of the Spirit through prayer and declaration of His Word, and then plunder the enemy's goods through proclaiming the good news to mankind and giving the opportunity of salvation. We must bear in mind that there may be times when the Lord calls on us to preach the gospel without much warning, leaving little time for prayer. However, even then, we must always remember that the gospel *is* the power of God, and will always bear fruit. Furthermore, we must learn to live a life of prayer (Smith Wigglesworth said, 'I never pray longer than thirty minutes; but thirty minutes never goes by when I am not praying!'), believe in the power of His Word, in the authority of His name, and that His Spirit is active in all the earth, calling His people into prayer at any and every moment. You can be assured that not only can *you* pray in faith and receive the answer, but someone, somewhere, prompted by the Spirit of God, is praying for you (not to mention *Jesus*, interceding at the right hand of the Father).

We must never give up in prayer, but keep pressing through on behalf of those without Christ. Paul, writing to the Galatians, said,

> '*My dear children, for whom I am **again** in the pains of childbirth, until Christ is formed in you ... '*
>
> (Galatians 4:19 NIV)

There is clearly both a bringing to birth in the Spirit, and a bringing forth of the life of Christ in His saints through such travail in the Spirit. Thus, our job is threefold: to bind the enemy through effective prayer warfare, to labour with the Holy Spirit (Romans 8:26) in bringing forth new souls for the Kingdom, and to bring the light and truth of the gospel that men and women might hear, believe and be saved.

## Releasing the power of the Kingdom

Our warfare is threefold: against the world, the flesh, and the devil. We defeat the world by applying the cross to our lives (Galatians 6:14), renewing our minds (Romans 12:1–2), loving the Father (a place of obedient worship, 1 John 2:15), and walking in faith (1 John 5:4–5). We overcome the flesh by walking in the Spirit (Galatians 5:16), leaning on grace (Romans 6:14), reckoning ourselves dead to sin through the finished work of Calvary (Romans 6:11), and saying '*no*' to ungodliness and lust (Titus 2:12). We overcome the devil by submitting to God and resisting the enemy (James 4:7), by applying the blood of the Lamb through the word of our testimony, and not loving our lives, even unto death (Revelation 12:11), by casting him out when we encounter him (Mark 16:17) and by being excellent in what is good (includes a walk of forgiveness), and innocent of evil, through which we are promised, '*the God of peace will crush Satan underneath your feet shortly*' (Romans 16:20 – how's that for meekness and militancy?).

Remember that the wonderful promises of God in Psalm 91 concerning protection are all conditional to living in 'the secret place', and that secret place is Christ ('*I will say of the Lord, "**He is my refuge**"*', v. 2). Abide in Christ through obedience to Him

(John 15:10). Confess any known sins, repent of them and put your faith in Christ to cleanse you from them through His precious blood. Make sure your relationships with other believers are right before God. We cannot claim to love God if we don't love our brothers (1 John 4:20), and if we hold unforgiveness against anyone we cannot be forgiven ourselves (Matthew 6:14–15), and indeed we become vulnerable to the enemy (Matthew 18:34–35). It is interesting to note that Carlos Anacondia, the great Argentinian evangelist, states that in his ministry's outreach to the demonised, approximately ninety per cent of all the people who come to them for help have problems with unforgiveness, bitterness or resentment in their lives. Let's learn to forgive and abide in the grace of God! According to 2 Corinthians 10:3–5, spiritual warfare is fought not only against the powers in the heavenlies, but most certainly against the strongholds that can be in our minds: unforgiveness, unbelief, cynicism, uncleanness, etc. These must be brought down by the power of the Word of God in our mouths, through repentance, forgiveness and humility.

Once we are in a place of right relationship with God and others, we can come against the enemy in the authority and power of the Lord Jesus Christ. To do this we need to have a strategy that is both spiritual and practical.

## Spiritual strategy

In our prayer warfare, we seek to utilise three of the most powerful tools given to us by God for victorious spiritual warfare. They are prayer, proclamation and praise. These are, if you like, the spiritual 'rocket-launchers' to our mighty 'warheads' of the name of Jesus, the blood of Jesus, and the Word of God, released with devastating effect on the enemy when spoken from believing lips!

In 2 Chronicles 20, in a time of national crisis, when Judah was surrounded by enemies, King Jehoshaphat gathered the people of God together in the temple where they called on the Lord for deliverance. The contents of the prayer prayed by Jehoshaphat, the prophetic declaration that followed, and the victorious praise that set the enemy into literal self-destruction are powerful lessons for us today (1 Corinthians 10:11). His prayer began with a declaration of the greatness of God (2 Chronicles 20:6), and then he continued by offering petition on the basis of his people's covenant with God (vv. 7–9: *not* on the basis of the need alone!), followed by a prophetic declaration of the purpose of God, on the basis of which the King proclaimed his faith in God's Word (vv. 14–17, 20). This all culminated in both spontaneous and orchestrated *praise* (vv. 21–22). It is interesting to note that, in verses 22–25, it was *when they began to praise* that the enemy was set into confusion, and literally self-destructed! It even took Judah (which means 'praise') three whole days to pick up all the spoils. Now that is victory! How true it is that 'the best way to defeat the demonic is to praise the divine!' (Judson Cornwall).

This principle is seen repeatedly in the Word of God. For example, on the Day of Pentecost, as the disciples gathered in unity in obedience to Jesus' word, there was united prayer, there was praise (in the Spirit!), and there was public declaration of the Word of God, leading to three thousand souls being added to the Church in one day. In the account of Paul and Silas in the Philippi prison, we discover that at midnight, despite the fact that they were chained up in the high-security jail and their backs were bleeding from the scourging they had suffered, they were heard *praying* and *singing hymns of praise* to God, until a great earthquake came and broke open all the doors, and all the chains just fell off (Acts 16 – isn't it amazing how our prayer and praise releases both ourselves and those around us from the enemy's chains?!!)! Paul proclaimed the gospel to the jailer and he and all his household were saved that night – and thus began the Philippian Church.

Of course, through the years that believers have been obeying the Great Commission, many have utilised this approach. John Wesley, the early Methodists, and the Salvation Army were some of the first to take their praise and prayer, testimony and preaching onto the streets, with great effect. In recent years, the wonderful 'Make Way' marches have also made much impact in many towns and cities around the globe.

## Practical strategy

We have found it very helpful, when praying in this way, to break up into groups of three or four. In each group the first person starts praying (in his/her own natural language), with the others coming into agreement (Matthew 18:19) and praying in the Spirit, followed by number two, then number three, etc., until the pray-ers are back to number one. They keep praying in a round like that until they sense a 'breakthrough' in the Spirit. Then we all begin to proclaim the promises of God over what we have prayed about, believing it is done (Mark 11:24), releasing the authority of the Word over the situation, and praising God for the answer! In a corporate setting this can be led from 'the front' or groups can be given a certain amount of autonomy to pray as the Spirit of God particularly directs them. We tend to pray around the particular outreach we are conducting at the time, as well as for unsaved friends, family, neighbours, the local churches and government, etc., and, in addition, coming against specific strongholds such as witchcraft.

Praying on the basis of the Word, we often use the pattern of New Testament prayers for evangelism, such as for good government that keeps the way open for public proclamation of the gospel (1 Timothy 2:1–4), open doors of opportunity to share the Word (Colossians 4:3), supernatural boldness (Acts 4:29), signs and wonders (Acts 4:30), for 'utterance' (that is, the words to communicate, Ephesians 6:19), and for labourers to be thrust forth into the harvest (Matthew 9:38). We have also often found it helpful to ask the Father to send out the angels (who minister to the heirs of salvation, Hebrews 1:14) to bring people across our paths that His Spirit has been preparing to receive the gospel. Finally, before going out to share the gospel on the streets or an outreach meeting, we regularly break bread together and share the wine, giving us opportunity to examine our hearts and make sure we are right with God, with one another, and that our focus of faith is clearly on the finished work of Calvary. Time after time, such praying has brought great spiritual breakthroughs, leading to many being saved, strongholds of witchcraft and rebellion being broken down and the Church coming together in unity, love and power to reach out to local communities with the good news of Jesus.

In closing this chapter we must briefly address the vital issue of bringing new converts through to true discipleship – lasting fruit. This is an issue so close to the heart of God that in John 21:15–17 we find Jesus effectively saying to Peter, "If you really love me, *feed* My sheep!" Such care for new believers is an evidence of love for God and if we are really going to destroy the enemy's spiritual hold on an area, we must combine the short-term impact of missions with the longer-term impact of church planting and true discipleship. Even the apostles saw the need of this as is highlighted in Acts 8 where Peter and John come to Samaria following Philip's evangelistic outreach there, in order to see the new converts established in the Spirit-filled life.

The evangelistic/apostolic connection that combines short-term impact and long-term fruit is powerful spiritual warfare! Without hesitation, I would say that the most fruitful outreaches we have ever conducted have been in the context of an apostolic vision, where mature leaders have trained up new leadership ready to plant a new church out of the evangelistic outreach being conducted in an area. May I suggest that to have two teams prepared in such an outreach is vital – one to evangelise, another to follow-up new converts the day after they have made their decision for Christ, inviting them to their homes, to church meetings etc., in order to establish relationship and teach them the fundamentals of God's Word. This is how effective disciples of Jesus are trained. In this way we will not only go into all the world and preach the Gospel, but we will be making disciples of all nations, partnering with Jesus as He builds His Church and advances His Kingdom in the earth.

Determine in your heart that you will never be a spectator in God's purposes, but an active participator. It's great going to conferences, reading books, listening to tapes: it all builds your faith (Romans 10:17), but if we never translate information into action, we will never live in the good of it! Our faith will be dead (James 2:17). The difference between teaching and training is application, experience. A soldier who knows everything about his weapon theoretically, but has never shot a bullet in his life is of little use on the battlefield! Take the challenge, embrace your call, have a *personal* testimony of spiritual exploits to the glory of God, and not just the re-collection of someone else's story.

Let's pray:

> Heavenly Father, I thank You for the privilege and honour of being called by You as a Priest and King unto My God, anointed to intercede, and to proclaim Your Kingdom to the ends of the earth. Lord, I take my place in Your great plan, I embrace my responsibility and receive Your anointing to accomplish the task You have set before me. I choose to be an active participator, not a passive observer! Strengthen Your Church, Lord, and the leaders You have appointed within her. Help us to walk in love, united in heart, moving forward in faith, and pressing on to fulfil Your Great Commission in our generation. May we always remember that to You, and You alone, belongs the Kingdom, the power and all the glory!
>
> In Jesus' precious name. Amen.

### Application

1. Define the nature of our warfare and weaponry (Ephesians 6:12; 2 Corinthians 10:3–4).

2. How do we receive what we desire in prayer (Mark 11:24)?

3. Explain the significance of man's authority on the earth, the effect of his submission/rebellion towards God in terms of spiritual warfare, and the necessity of intercessory prayer (see section on 'Whose world is it?').

4. Name the three powerful tools the Lord has given us (there are others such as testimony, fasting, etc.) in releasing our spiritual weaponry against the enemy. How is this illustrated in the biblical accounts of 2 Chronicles 20, Acts 2 and Acts 16?

5. What part do the angels play in spiritual warfare and evangelism (Daniel 10; Hebrews 1:14; Acts 8:26; 10:3)?

# Chapter 7

# Turning the World 'Upside Down'

It has been said that if Christians truly believed the message they preach, they would change the world overnight! However, such a change would inevitably bring the Church of Jesus Christ into direct confrontation with the world, a confrontation we need to be prepared for since Jesus Himself prophesied this would be so (Mark 13:13). In Acts 17, when Paul and Silas began preaching the gospel in Thessalonica, there was such an uproar that those who opposed their ministry dragged some of the believers to the rulers of the city crying out, *'these who have **turned the world upside down** have come here too'* (v. 6). What a glorious indictment! This lost world needs 'turning upside down' (or, rather, 'the right way up'). What was it about their message that made such an impact? Verse 7 tells us, *'these are all acting contrary to the decrees of Caesar, saying **there is another King – Jesus.'*** According to Romans 13:1 we are required by God to be subject to the governing authorities of our nations. Nevertheless, when civil law contradicts Kingdom law, we are faced with no other alternative but to submit to the Word of God and stand up for Jesus against the tide of ungodliness and sin, whether it be expressed in personal behaviour or be enshrined in governmental legislation (see Acts 4:1–33). There are times when obedience to God means disobedience to the civil authorities. The apostles didn't try to 'fit in' or be somehow 'relevant' to the culture: they literally confronted and transformed it, and without question their ministry was effective. Although there was great opposition stirred up by the enemy (working through the unbelief and envy of those who would not receive the Word of God), Scripture tells us,

> 'And some of them were persuaded and **a great multitude** of the devout Greeks, and not a few of the leading women, joined Paul and Silas.' (Acts 17:4)

In his first letter to the Thessalonians, Paul, describing their conversion to Christ, said,

> 'For our gospel did not come to you in word only, but also in power, and in the Holy Spirit, and in much assurance ... And you became followers of us and of the Lord, having received the word in much affliction, with joy of the Holy Spirit ... ' (1 Thessalonians 1:5–6)

You tell a tree by its fruit! Some believers today, encountering such opposition, would think that maybe they had taken the wrong approach, that maybe they ought to present the gospel in a more 'gentle' or 'sensitive' way. But we need to face the fact that the days are soon coming when to proclaim the uniqueness of Christ and the authority of His Kingdom in the pluralistic culture of the Western world could be costly in the same ways that many of our brothers and sisters in other parts of the world have had to endure for years. National revival in the Church and resultant awakening in the world will be unlikely without sacrifice. It is time to establish clearly whom we will serve, where we stand in terms of righteousness before God, and the cost we are willing to pay for what we believe.

Returning to our passage in Acts 17, although Paul and Silas had to move on to Berea (where they just carried on preaching the same gospel in the same way but this time with a different response: note that it is *not* us who need to change the message, but the world that needs to be changed by the unchanging message of the gospel of Christ!), God started a wonderful work in Thessalonica, out of which was born a new church. While it is vitally true that in these days the Lord is seeking to break down the four walls of our churches, so that we begin to connect with those who don't know Christ in every aspect of life – business, the arts, education, etc. – it is fundamental that we do not lose sight of the fact that *the work of the gospel is not to make God acceptable to men, but men acceptable to God, through Christ!*

## A culturally relevant/seeker-friendly message?

In many Western churches today it has almost become the expected 'norm' to ensure that every presentation of the gospel is 'seeker-sensitive', or at least 'culturally-relevant'. While recognising the value in using all manner of presentation to communicate the gospel to every generation and culture (not *only* 'youth' culture) in such a way that we dismantle the negative concepts that have built up in some people's minds as to what Christianity is all about, thus giving them every opportunity to be saved, it is vital that we do not forget that Jesus, the Lord of every nation (*ethnos*) in the world, knows exactly how to reach every culture on the planet! It is interesting to note that in His instructions to His disciples on how to reach the world with the gospel, there is no such teaching mentioned. However, He did say,

> *'As you go, preach, saying, "The Kingdom of heaven is at hand." Heal the sick, cleanse the lepers, raise the dead, cast out demons.'*
> (Matthew 10:7)

Jesus underlined this approach again in His declaration in Mark 16, when describing the ministry of believers as they go into *all the world* preaching the gospel:

> *'And these signs will follow those who believe: In My name they will cast out demons; they will speak with new tongues ... they will lay hands on the sick and they will recover.'*
> (Mark 16:17–18)

I remember preaching the gospel on the streets in Ukraine when a woman who had been healed of blindness, deafness and arthritis in our meetings the day before broke through the crowd of people who had gathered to hear us preach and told them all, 'Listen to these men! They are not telling you Western political dogma, they are here to tell you about Jesus. Look at me! You all know that I was blind and deaf, that you had to help me down the steps from my flat because I could not walk . . . Now I can see, I can hear, I can walk. Listen to them; it is true – Jesus is alive!' It was not difficult to preach after such a testimony, and forty people gave their lives to Christ on the spot, with the result that within days a new church was planted in that area to care for these new believers. It is the gospel, preached with a certain and faith-filled conviction, that God confirms with signs following, reaching every culture and every generation on the face of the planet.

## Culture is more than style

*The Chambers Dictionary* defines 'culture' as 'the attitudes and values which inform a society'. With Western attitudes and values being what they are, i.e. totally godless, humanistic and at best relativistic in their outlook (i.e. without any absolutes), it really begs the question, 'Is God (the true and only God, as revealed in Jesus Christ) relevant at all to those who do not know Him in the secularised culture of the Western world?' For those focused on 'keeping in step' with the cultures of this world, adjusting their churches, preaching, ministry, etc., to become more 'inclusive', there are some very serious questions to be asked. In much the same way as humanism has paved the way for Islam in the modern Western nations (when Christianity is certainly not tolerated in Islamic nations!), we need to be very careful that the message of 'cultural relevance' does not pave the way for pluralism, liberalism, relativistic values and even the incredibly dangerous 'playing down' of some Christian leaders of the occultic nature of some of the influences affecting our children and youth today, such as the 'Harry Potter' books (to name but one obvious example of the way the enemy has been infiltrating a Church that is half asleep to the dangers that are even now working as a 'Fifth Column' within the ranks of those called by the name of 'Christian'). The real danger is that the enemy, who is a long-term strategist, is aiming at the internal weakening of the Church's value-system and convictions of the absolute authority of Scripture, and of eternal and moral truth. Consequently, when the real battles against the uniqueness of

Christ, against the uniqueness of the Holy Bible as the only inerrant and absolute Word of God, etc., come through false religion and humanism, bringing a genuine threat to freedom of worship and proclamation of the gospel in the Western world, the Church will lack the moral fibre and strength of conviction to stand up to the enemy's onslaught. There is a genuine war on for the very 'soul' of the Church at this time, and it is seductively quiet and deceptive. (But challenge it and see how noisy it will become!) It's time for the Church, which is *'the pillar and ground of the truth'* (1 Timothy 3:15), to rise up and infiltrate the world, presenting a clear, radical and godly alternative to the rubbish the world presents as 'normality'. We are the light of the world, the salt of the earth, a city set on a hill – distinct, different, standing out, showing forth in our lives and words the solid ground of Truth upon which a healthy society can be built, and the life-changing power of the grace of God, by which a broken one can be healed! If we fail to address these issues in the Church now, we will soon find there to be a distinct lack of moral fibre, heart conviction and true leadership in the Body of Christ that will leave the next generation terribly vulnerable to deception as it faces the challenges of a pluralistic, humanistic society threatened by fundamentalist Muslims and militant homosexuality!

I fully understand that what I am saying may come as somewhat of a shock to you, the reader, but just to allay your fears that you might be reading something a little too extreme, let me give you a few further examples of the way this 'approach/belief system' is affecting the Church. On a number of occasions, in different Western countries, I have had the unpleasant experience of hearing a Christian leader swear, or take the name of God in vain in my presence, only to have it justified as 'only cultural'! I have to ask, 'When did culture become a valid biblical excuse for blasphemy and profanity?' What about Ephesians 4:29: *'Let no corrupt word proceed out of your mouth, but what is good for necessary edification, that it may impart grace to the hearers?'* On another occasion, in Eastern Europe, I was told by an apostolic leader, with some concern, that a brother in ministry from the West shared how they had had such an impact on the youth of their nation. When asked what he saw as being the key to such success, the brother replied, 'We seek to be "culturally relevant".' His response to my friend's enquiry as to what this meant I found somewhat devastating. The brother replied, 'For example, we don't use the Bible much in our youth gatherings, because the Bible is "culturally irrelevant" to young people!' And this at a time when England has the highest teen pregnancy and abortion figures in Europe! At a time when 50 per cent of marriages are over in the first five years and children grow up in a fatherless society, hating the authority figures they encounter because the Father who should have been there to give them healthy discipline and boundaries in life walked out on them, or was walked out on by their mother! How tragic that such people, so desperate to be found 'relevant' to their culture, seem so easily to forget that people gave their lives to give us the Word of God, and such sacrifice was made at a time when to have the Scriptures in one's own language was considered irrelevant – at least by the leaders of the religious community. The dangers in such an approach are obvious and potentially catastrophic in their implications for both the Church and the world she is called to win for Christ.

If the line is not clearly drawn between issues of style/ presentation, etc., and the value system/attitudes of the human- istic society in which we live, we are in grave danger of exchang- ing the biblical values of moral righteousness for tolerated immorality and living for the moment, justified by sentiments such as, 'It feels right' and 'God wants me to be happy and enjoy myself, doesn't He?', and pacified by, 'It's OK, there's grace and forgiveness'. But mercy without truth is meaningless! This all may seem extreme, but it is sadly too common to be ignored. We need to face the fact that the line between embracing the style and 'ethos' of a culture in order to reach that culture, and embracing its values and attitudes is 'paper-thin'. Leaders carry a great responsibility in bringing crystal-clear definition of the boundaries – for the sake of God's glory, of the state of Christ's Bride, the Church, and of our responsibility to present clearly the saving gospel of Christ without compromise to a world that is lost in sin.

There are other, more subtle influences, too: freedom for the

Holy Spirit to direct the ministry of Christ in His Church being exchanged for structure, planning and format (don't get me wrong, I know there's a place for all that, but *not* at the expense of the Spirit's sovereignty in a gathering). Some seem to be more concerned with the quality of the presentation and music than they are in the quality of the worship! May the Lord open our eyes to see beyond mere external form, and restore us (as we respond in repentance) to true worship, uncompromised ministry of the Word, and sensitivity to the Holy Spirit. Then we will truly see the unsaved responding to the presence of God, 'falling down and worshipping God exclaiming, "God is really among you!"' It's one thing to hold to 'incarnational theology' believing we need to present Jesus to the world in a way that people can relate to – as He did by becoming man – but some seem to have forgotten the supernatural dynamic that He *'went about doing good, and healing all who were oppressed of the devil, for God was with Him'* (Acts 10:38). Have we compromised the true image of Christ for a Christ who fits our comfortable, politically correct culture?

## You are relevant!

While it is obviously true that the 'packaging' in which the gospel is presented is in many ways a neutral and negotiable issue (provided that it does not take away from the gospel itself nor cross biblical standards of righteousness and truth), the great concern is that, in some instances, the true message of the gospel is not being clearly presented, nor an adequate challenge to commit one's life to Christ in repentance and faith being given. Great bridges are being built with communities, but saints seem unwilling to truly confront with the gospel, and thus bring people over the bridge into the Kingdom of God. But what good is a bridge that nobody crosses?!

It is tragic that at a time when the need for the Church of Jesus Christ to rise up and proclaim the gospel with true Holy Spirit boldness to our land is unprecedented, many churches in the West are caught in a side-alley by the enemy, constantly trying to find out how they may become somehow 'relevant' to their culture. Churches are desperately concerned that if they are not relevant in their approach, according to the expression deemed relevant by those who promote such a message, then they are in the serious position of being considered 'irrelevant' (since there is no 'middle ground' here!) and therefore useless in terms of reaching anyone with the gospel! The truth is, there may well be some things stylistically that we can and should change, and provided something is not sinful we should certainly recognise that 'different' is not necessarily 'wrong', and may even assist in the dismantling of religious stereotypes in the minds of un-believers, thus making a way for them to take a further step towards salvation without unnecessary barriers of unbiblical Church traditions and culture (there are some 'biblical' ones!) standing in the way. However, to make the 'packaging' such a focus was *never* Jesus' intention for the Church. If you are saved, you *are* relevant! You have the answer! Ultimately, people are more interested in the reality of God in your life than in the style of your hair, the choice of your clothes, or the music that you play (they already have the styles, fashions and music of the world anyway)! Everyone on the planet needs forgiveness, love, acceptance, an assurance of eternal life – the moment someone gives his or her life to Jesus Christ, he or she immediately becomes supremely relevant to every culture in every people group, anywhere in the world.

## Pleasing God or pleasing people?

It is one thing to be sensitive to those who may come into our church services, seeking to know more about the Lord, but it is another thing entirely when we lose our 'cutting edge' in the gospel through trying to be so sensitive to people's views and wishes that we are no longer pleasers of God but pleasers of people! The effect of this on our faith walk can be devastating. In the words of Jesus,

> *'How can you **believe**, who receive honour from one another, and do not seek the honour that comes from the only God?'*
>
> (John 5:44)

We should be seeking the Word of the Lord concerning how to reach those without Christ, and acting in faith on His Word rather than constantly being preoccupied with how we can better relate to the culture around us (a culture that is constantly changing and doomed to perish, 1 John 2:17).

This very same truth can certainly also be applied to leaders who gather in an expression of unity for the sake of mutual fellowship and support. If the full power of Christ's Body coming together is going to be realised in terms of the salvation of our communities and nations (John 17:21), we cannot afford merely to gather around the lowest common denominator, developing a unity based on compromise that lacks any real united power in prayer or common initiative producing corporate growth for the Kingdom of God. While there is clearly value in creating a forum for the fostering of true unity, if in the pursuit of unity we lose our sharpness in the Word of God, and fail to see the release of the Spirit's power to accomplish the purposes of God, we will find ourselves in a compromised position, missing the high calling of God and failing to honour His name and Word above the fleeting opinions of our fellow human beings.

Paul states in Galatians 1:10, *'if I still pleased men, I would not be a bondservant of Christ'*. The two are mutually exclusive. Later, in 5:11, defending the message of the gospel of grace, he says, *'if I still preach circumcision* [which would have been the acceptable message in the Jewish culture of his day], *why do I still suffer persecution? Then the offence of the cross has ceased.'* It is not our aim deliberately to offend anyone, but if our message produces no offence at all, we have to question whether we are really preaching the true gospel of Christ. It was Jesus who said,

> *'Blessed are you when men hate you, and when they exclude you, and revile you, and cast out your name as evil, for the Son of Man's sake. Rejoice in that day and leap for joy! For indeed your reward is great in heaven, for in like manner their fathers did to the prophets ... Woe to you when all men speak well of you, for so did their fathers to **the false** prophets.'*        (Luke 6:22–23, 26)

The famous English preacher and founder of the Methodist

movement, John Wesley, used to say that if he went through more than a few days without being assaulted, insulted or persecuted in some way as he travelled around England preaching the gospel, he began to wonder if he was in some way 'backslidden' or had somehow compromised the message of the cross. May God so move in our hearts that we are more concerned for His glory than for our safety! I long for the day when the streets of our nation are filled again with the sounds of praise, of tears shed in repentance, and the gospel being preached with faith, passion and full conviction; where preachers are not hidden behind the relative safety of a church pulpit within four walls, but are out where the people are, where Jesus preached and ministered, healing hearts and changing lives.

## The culture of the King

Jesus told us to go and proclaim, *'The kingdom of heaven is at hand'* (Matthew 10:7). There is another King, another Kingdom, and one day the kingdoms of this world will become the kingdoms of our Lord and Christ. Our citizenship is in heaven, and we are to emulate the attitudes and values (the never-changing culture) of that Kingdom here upon the earth, thus being salt and light to society at large.

One of the attitudes in our present Western culture that has done great damage both in society at large and in the Church is the attitude of disrespect (which sometimes translates into rebellion when it is not curbed) towards those in authority. While it is true that much of this attitude is rooted in rejection and a deep reaction to the failure of fathers to love their children, be faithful to their wives and lead their homes in godly conduct, it is none the less true that we do not have to let our history control our destiny! There is grace in God for forgiveness, as we repent, embrace our new identity in Christ, and walk in the love of our great Father-God! We really can learn to receive and live under authority, thus being able to exercise God-given authority (Matthew 8:5–13), and receive the benefits that such authority bestows. The effect of choosing to believe, choosing to respect and receive God-given authority in our lives is dynamic. The consequences of not doing so are tragic. This is clearly seen in the context of Jesus' ministry to His own home town. In Matthew 13:54–58 we see that, despite His miracles and wise words, the people were offended at Him, being disrespectful to His office and call in God, saying, *'Is this not the carpenter's son? Is not His mother called Mary?'* The Bible records,

> *'Now He did not do many mighty works there **because of their unbelief.'***          (Matthew 13:58)

The people knew Him naturally, related to Him naturally, but failed to recognise, respect and honour His divine calling. Thus, there was much unbelief and few miracles. Sadly, this is the case in many a church in the Western world. A culture of disrespect is a culture of unbelief! Authority, respect, faith and miracles go hand in hand! It is time that we started to honour and respect the ministries God has given us, letting go of some of our over-familiarity and learning to receive from the God-given authority and anointing that He has placed in our leaders. It is time for younger generation leaders to respect, learn from and serve the 'spiritual fathers' of the previous generation that there may be a genuine impartation of authority and anointing of spiritual leadership. Nowhere in Scripture do we find impartation of anointing from one generation to another without a significant period of service, humility and proven faithfulness to the generation God raised up before (consider Moses/Joshua, Elijah/Elisha, Paul/Timothy). The embracing of biblical values and attitudes brings biblical blessings, anointing and results.

Let us remember that it is through the cross that we die to the world and the world dies to us (Galatians 6:14). This message that we preach is a direct confrontation to this world's system and values, and indeed to Satan himself, who is its god (2 Corinthians 4:4). When we try to reach people on the basis of their culture to the extent that their culture becomes the dictating influence to our calling, ministry, and life in God, we become slaves to the spirit that is behind it and our ministry becomes ineffective for reaching those lost in its grip. We are called to declare and demonstrate the presence of another culture, another Kingdom, another King! It was Dr Martyn Lloyd-Jones who stated, 'When the Church is so obviously different from the world, she invariably attracts her.' Some long-term missionaries, while starting out well, have ended up in a state of unfruitfulness, totally ineffective for reaching the people to whom they were sent, because they have become 'part of the scenery'. Instead of becoming *'like'* (not 'the same as') *'that I might by all means save some'* (1 Corinthians 9:19–23), they've just become 'like'. They have lost their cutting edge and now are forever preoccupied with building bridges with their communities (all valid in and of itself), without bringing anyone over the bridges they have created. This leaves the world as lost as it ever was, and the Church in a state of discouragement, afraid to confront with the gospel in case anyone might be 'put off' and thereby lost. It is a grave deception to believe that we can somehow reach the lost by 'being the gospel' without ever truly proclaiming it! That dear old saint who declared to his followers, 'Preach the gospel everywhere, and if necessary, use words' could not have read his Bible that states so categorically, *'how shall they believe in Him of whom they have not heard?'* (Romans 10:13). Such teaching is counter-productive for the cause of Christ, producing much barrenness for the work of the gospel in many Western churches. Whereas we all recognise that there is both *process* and *crisis* in evangelism, if it is *only* the 'process' approach that people hear, believers can easily be led into a place where they are (1) afraid to confront with the gospel (therefore unable to bring someone into a personal relationship with Christ through repentance and faith), and (2) afraid to move on from those who will not receive the gospel, just in case through their long enduring relationship the unsaved person might just give their lives to Christ one day. In the meantime, there may be hundreds of unsaved people being lost to God for eternity who could have been reached through the witness of that well-meaning believer. In my own ministry in evangelism over the last fourteen years, I have had to learn, sometimes painfully, that Satan is a past-master at creating 'red-herrings' (bringing people into your life or ministry who are just wasting your time, 'sent' to 'wear down the saints', with no genuine intention of ever giving their lives to Christ). We must keep our ears open to heaven, and our focus clear on the mission Christ has given us. The scripture is plain, *'My Spirit shall not strive with man forever . . . '* (Genesis 6:3). Jesus said,

> *'But whatever city you enter, and they do not receive you, go out into its streets and say, "The very dust of your city which clings to us we wipe off against you. Nevertheless know this, that the Kingdom of God has come near you." But I say to you that it will be more tolerable in that Day* [of judgement] *for Sodom than for that city.'* (Luke 10:10–12)

I am by no means advocating that we withdraw from the unsaved (Jesus was 'the friend of sinners'), nor that we cease to *'by all means save some'*, but I am urging us not to lose our focus, our urgency, and indeed our message in the midst of the packaging with which we seek to present it. We are called and commissioned by the God who is love, who sends us *into* all the world, *into* their cultures, their lives, not to embrace or be limited by their values and belief systems, but to see them wonderfully saved and transformed by the grace and power of God. We must recognise that we are in a war for souls, a war that is waged against 'the god of this world' who has created his own false reality that those without Christ relate to as 'reality'. It is what Isaiah called 'the veil that lies over the nations', and what Satan uses to 'blind the minds of unbelievers' (2 Corinthians 4:4). It is only when we, through prayer, bind his activity and through preaching the gospel bring light (the entrance of His Word brings light) into their hearts and lives, that people are able to 'see' the truth (reality), believe in Jesus, and thus be saved. We are not to present the glorious gospel of Christ as 'the Christian view' (which would be falling prey to humanistic relativism), but as the absolute Word of God which effectively works in those who believe. The very declaration of that Word is confrontational spiritual warfare against the god of this age. It is the *rhema* of God, the 'spoken Word' which is *'the sword of the Spirit'* (Ephesians 6:17), that cuts through that deceptive veil and reveals the heavenly realities of eternal truth that sets people free in Jesus Christ.

Let's pray:

> Father, I thank You that You have saved us *out of* every tongue tribe and nation, to be a Kingdom of Priests unto You. Thank You that You have given us the great opportunity and privilege to go right back into these very cultures and people groups to be Your representatives, proclaiming and demonstrating Your values, Your grace and Your power to those who don't yet know You. Lord, please forgive me for the times when I have embraced attitudes and values that were not the values of Your Kingdom, when I have limited the work of Your Spirit through unbelief and fear of man. I truly repent and commit myself to You afresh, and the ministry to which You have called me. Let my life and ministry truly be a full expression of Your Kingdom, Your love, Your holiness, and Your power. I make a quality decision today to believe Your Word rather than the circumstances around me, to live in obedience to You, and take every opportunity You give me. I will not concern myself with the opinions of my fellow human beings, but I devote myself to pleasing You and doing Your will, Your Way.
>
> In Jesus' name, Amen.

## Application

1. How would you describe yourself: someone who passively accepts the 'status quo', or someone who actively seeks, through your intercession and witness, to bring the values and power of the Kingdom of God into every facet of life that you encounter?

2. What can we learn about Jesus' approach in winning the people of this world to Himself from Matthew 10:7–8 and Mark 16:15–20?

3. To what extent has your faith, practice of ministry, lifestyle and value system been influenced and affected by the values and attitudes of the culture around you? If necessary, come in repentance and renewed commitment to Christ and His Kingdom values that your focus may be sharpened, and your faith released to walk in a lifestyle and ministry that is shaped by Him rather than by the cultures of this world.

4. Is there a place for becoming 'like' in order to see people saved, without embracing the values and attitudes of this world (1 Corinthians 9:19–23)? Think of some concrete examples.

5. Is there anyone in your life with whom you have built relationship but never truly challenged with the gospel? If so, ask God for the opportunity to do so, and then take it when it comes.

# Chapter 8

# Strength for the Battle
# (Supernatural Sustenance)

'Burned out', 'stressed out', 'dropped out': these are terms we hear in the ministry all too often. The numbers of leaders dropping out of ministry today in some parts of the world is alarming – particularly at a time when the battle is 'hotting up' and the harvest is so great. We must learn to live close to Christ, the source of life, faith, strength and anointing so that we not only experience short-term victories, but achieve our long-term destinies in God. We are privileged in our day to experience regular outpourings of the Holy Spirit, but we must learn not only to 'ride the wave' when it comes, but live at the source!

None of the teaching contained here denies the reality of our need for proper rest, a healthy diet and regular exercise (we are spirit, soul and body), nor should we ever think that we can live in sin and still expect divine life! All sin carries an element of death in its wake (Romans 6:23), and it is interesting to note that the Hebrew word for 'iniquity' even has the connotation of 'exhaustion', something to which Psalm 32:3–5 clearly alludes. Nonetheless, the ministry to which God has called each one of us is in essence a spiritual work that can ultimately only be accomplished with spiritual power, and we must learn to find supernatural sustenance in the presence of God if we are ever going to have the strength to see the fullness of God's purpose fulfilled through our lives. The apostle John states,

> 'Beloved, I pray that you may prosper and be in health, **just as your soul prospers.**'
> (3 John 2)

James reminds us that the body *'without the spirit'* is dead (James

2:26). And Paul encourages Timothy that he has not been given *'a **spirit** of fear, but a **spirit** of power, love and a sound, calm, and well-balanced mind'* (2 Timothy 1:7 Amplified Version). Clearly the source of our strength, wholeness, stability and success is spiritual. In much the same way as internal foundations determine the outward strength of a physical building, if our inner life is strong in God, the outer life will follow suite, but if the inner life is weak through lack of spiritual sustenance in the presence of God by His Word and Spirit, sooner or later the cracks will start to show under the pressure of the trials and temptations of life and ministry!

## Sustained by His presence

The principle of supernatural sustenance, strength and life flowing into and affecting our human frame is clearly presented in both the Old and New Testaments, and is fully available for us today.

Moses spent forty days and forty nights in the direct presence of God, neither eating bread nor drinking water (Exodus 34:28–30)! A physical impossibility (at least without drinking water). He was supernaturally sustained by the direct, manifest presence of God. (I would certainly *not* recommend you trying to follow this exact pattern, particularly not drinking water for an extended period. This is an exceptional case, initiated by God Himself out of a 'face to face' encounter with Moses, Exodus 33:11.) When Moses descended from the mountain he didn't realise that his face was literally shining with the glory of God, which made the people frightened to come near him. This very same principle is seen in the New Testament, when Jesus was transfigured (Greek, *metamorphoo*: to change into another form, from which we get the English word 'metamorphosis') (Mark 9:2–13).

> *'His clothes became white, like snow, such as no launderer on earth can whiten them.'*     (v. 3)

Following this occurrence, Scripture tells us,

> *'Immediately, when they saw Him, all the people were greatly amazed, and running to Him, greeted Him.'*     (Mark 9:15)

They would have seen the glory of God upon Him, just as it had been upon Moses, except this time the glory did not come with the bondage to fear that the law brings, but with the freedom of grace,

> *'For the law was given through Moses, but grace and truth came through Jesus Christ.'*                    (John 1:17)

Hence, they were not afraid to approach Him. It is also interesting to note that it was in this context that Jesus dealt with the deaf and dumb spirit that the disciples couldn't cast out. From the high place of glory in the manifest presence of His Father, He came into the valley of their doubts and fears bringing the power of deliverance by the Spirit of God. When answering the disciples' questions concerning the event, He answered, *'This kind can come out by nothing but prayer and fasting'* (v. 29) – exactly what He had been doing!

Of further interest is the fact that according to Paul, speaking by the Spirit of God in 2 Corinthians 3:18, we are also *'transformed'* (*metamorphoo* – same Greek word), not so much by our own efforts as by beholding, through grace (an *unveiled* face!), the glory (substance, weightiness, revelation) of the Lord. In that very place of intimacy with God, we are changed to be like Him, from one degree of glory to another, and that by the Spirit of God! How many times have we experienced this liberty, this transforming grace, when once we have stopped striving and simply entered His presence! Have you not seen that look of 'glory' on the faces of those who have truly entered into His presence in worship and encountered Him? No wonder in the East African Revival, those brothers and sisters who spent long hours in the presence of God, were known as 'the shining ones'. Their faces literally reflected the glory of the God they had been beholding in heartfelt worship and intercession.

## On 'wings like eagles'

Isaiah declared the word of the Lord to those downcast at not yet seeing the breakthrough, the answer to prayer, they had been looking for:

*'Have you not known?*
*Have you not heard?*
*The everlasting God, the* Lord,
*The Creator of the ends of the earth*
*Neither faints, nor is weary.*
*His understanding is unsearchable.*
*He gives power to the weak,*
*And to those who have no might He increases strength.*
*Even the youths shall faint and be weary,*
*And the young men shall utterly fall,*
*But those who **wait** [in faith – Hebrew emphasis]*
    **on the Lord**
*Shall renew their strength;*
*They shall mount up with wings like eagles,*
*They shall run and not be weary,*
*They shall walk and not faint.'*                    (Isaiah 40:28–31)

Here the prophet is making an obvious reference to the way eagles fly up to the high mountains to stretch out their wings in the sun where they are renewed so that they are able to soar in the heights once more. We can be renewed in His presence! A number of times I have been out in the bush, somewhere in Africa or Asia, exhausted or sick from some tropical bug, and turned my eyes toward heaven, raised my voice in praise to God, and experienced His healing and refreshing presence restore, heal and strengthen me again to go back out to win the lost and bring that very same life-changing, miracle-working presence of God into the needy lives to whom we were ministering. Praise God for His great promises – there is an endless supply of life and strength in the presence of God if we will only come and receive, come and drink of the rivers that never run dry.

## The ministry of Jesus

Jesus declared that He could of Himself do nothing. The things that He did were the things that He *saw* His Father doing first (John 5:19). His 'secret' was that His ministry flowed out of *relationship* with the Father. Where, as ministers, we might receive prophetic discernment/vision/words of knowledge concerning what God is going to do in a particular meeting/aspect of ministry, and then by acting on that in faith see God break out in the miraculous amongst us, Jesus functioned like that every moment of every day! And it is *that* fellowship and function that we have all been called into by Christ (see 1 John 1:3; 2:6). He met with His Father in 'the secret place' of prayer, and the Father rewarded Him openly with the answers to His prayers. He petitioned in the secret place and released the answers to those petitions (which He had received in the secret place through faith and with directions from the Father by the Spirit) in public. Hence His public 'ministry prayers' were short (i.e., 'receive your sight', 'stretch forth your arm', etc.). Words of command spoken in faith releasing in the natural what He had received in the secret place by the Spirit! In Luke 5:15–16 we read,

> ' ... *multitudes came together to hear and be healed by Him of their infirmities. So He Himself **often** withdrew into the wilderness and prayed.*'

It was there that He received the strength, anointing and wisdom from His Father for each step in His ministry. When it came time to choose His apostles, He spent all night in personal prayer (Luke 6:12–13 – would to God that more ministries would do that today! We would certainly have less problems in the ministry). He knew exactly whom to choose on the basis of His Father's 'foreknowledge' and, furthermore, the overflow of that intimacy with His Father was a dynamic release of manifest healing power that caused the whole multitude of people there to seek to touch Him *'for power went out from Him and healed them **all**'* (Luke 6:19). I can remember times when out of a deep personal encounter with God the miraculous has flowed with such ease and power that literally everyone to whom I had the privilege of ministering was instantly healed. It didn't seem to matter what the condition was: arthritis, deafness, cancer – one after another, they would be instantly healed! We must learn to give ourselves to God in a wholehearted seeking of His face, His presence, His power, staying in the place of humble, dependent, faith-filled confidence in our wonderful Redeemer, with *whom all things are possible!*

Jesus warned us that in the last days we should take heed to ourselves, lest our hearts be 'weighed down' (causing spiritual dullness and inability to perceive and hear the word of the Lord and recognise the seasons of God) with carousing (we could say 'general immorality'), drunkenness, and the *cares of this life*, and that Day come on you unexpectedly (Luke 21:34). Jesus always lived what He preached and He gave us the perfect example of how to stand firm under pressure. In Luke 22:39–46, just before His betrayal by Judas, Jesus knelt down and prayed, submitting Himself to the Father's will. An angel from heaven appeared from heaven to assist/strengthen Him. Scripture clearly says, *'being in agony, He prayed more earnestly.'* No wonder James later wrote, *'Is anyone among you suffering? Let him pray'* (James 5:13). However, the disciples, despite Jesus' inferred warning that if they didn't pray they would enter into temptation, were *'sleeping from sorrow'* (Luke 22:45: they were emotionally exhausted). Again He repeated His exhortation, *'Why do you sleep? Rise and pray, **lest you enter into temptation'** (v. 46). Personal prayer is a place of victory over temptation, of submission to the Father, of angelic assistance, and release from negative emotions! Note that both Paul (Philippians 4:4–7) and Peter (1 Peter 5:6–7) underline exactly the same principle. We must learn to cast our cares on the Lord in the humility that acknowledges we cannot overcome without Him, and the faith that thankfully recognises we are **not** without Him, and chooses to rejoice with a sacrifice of praise, offering its petition to our faithful God who is always present and just waiting to carry that burden away in answered prayer.

## The Elijah syndrome

The account of the battle between Elijah and Jezebel's false prophets on Mount Carmel (1 Kings 18:41 – 19:1–18) is another powerful illustration of this principle of supernatural sustenance. Every step that Elijah took was directed by the Spirit of God: the challenge to the false prophets and indeed to Israel, the fire that fell and consumed the sacrifice, altar and even the water in the trench, the ending of the drought. It was all by the word of the Lord (1 Kings 18:36). Elijah could act with great boldness, even telling his servant to look out to the horizon seven times for the cloud of rain that he had seen coming in his spirit before it could be seen naturally. Acting on the word of the Lord, he was seeing miracles birthed/released in the natural world, even running faster than a chariot as a result of the Spirit of God coming upon him (1 Kings 18:46). All of these things were initiated by the Spirit of God and released as Elijah acted obediently in faith. However, when he heard the threats of Jezebel he was afraid and *'ran for his life'* (the scripture says, *'when he saw that'* [v. 3]: her words painted an inner image of fear and destruction in much the same way that the word of the Lord had painted an inner image of the fire falling, rain coming, etc., producing faith and boldness in Elijah – we must learn to 'take captive' such thoughts, 2 Corinthians 10:3–5). It is following this account that we read of Elijah being exhausted, wanting to die, and going into the wilderness and on to Horeb (which in Hebrew means 'desolation'). It is often after times of great anointing, of great victories, when we are physically/emotionally exhausted that the enemy attacks, and it is then that we need to come straight back into the presence of God to be strengthened again, lest we fall prey to the enemy's devices. Thank God that even in the midst of Elijah's flight from Jezebel, there was supernatural provision (1 Kings 19:5–8) in the form of two meals prepared by an angel! There is a clear inference here that Elijah's flight was not the will of God for him (*'What are you doing here, Elijah?'*, 1 Kings 19:9, 13), and it was as a result of these incidents that Elijah is taken out of his front-line confrontational role and given a new (but brief!) ministry to raise up the next generation of prophets and kings before he is taken to glory (possibly prematurely). Many lessons can be learned from this passage by us today as the war between the spirit of Jezebel and the end-time Elijah generation (preparing the way of the Lord, Malachi 4:5) rages. We must learn to guard our hearts with the Word of God as well as be led by, and full of, the Spirit of God.

## Faith's renewal

There are many vital things that God has given us as keys to renewal in our personal lives and ministry and, in one sense, following in the footsteps of Jesus means a process of ongoing death and resurrection, of divine renewal (Luke 9:23–24; 1 Corinthians 15:31; 2 Corinthians 1:3–4, 8–11). In fact, this principle (i.e. that out of death comes life) is the very principle that the principalities and powers did not understand, for otherwise they would not have crucified the Lord of glory (1 Corinthians 2:8)! The apostle Paul understood it well,

> *'And He said to me, "My grace* [Greek, charis] *is sufficient for you, for My strength* [Greek, dunamis – miracle-working power/ability] *is made perfect in your weakness* [inability to produce results]." *Therefore, most gladly will I rather boast in my infirmities, that the power* [dunamis – there it is again!] *of Christ may rest upon me … For when I am weak, then I am strong.'* (2 Corinthians 12:9–10)

It all flows from the source of our life, who is Christ (1 John 5:11–12).

In 2 Corinthians 4:7–18 Paul outlines this very principle, acknowledging that we have the treasure of divine life and anointing in *earthen* vessels. This is the great 'but' of faith:

> *'We are hard-pressed on every side,* **yet** *not crushed; we are perplexed,* **but** *not in despair; persecuted* **but** *not forsaken … '* (2 Corinthians 4:8–9)

There is a 'but' of doubt ('I know what God's promises say, *but …* '), and a 'but' of faith ('I know what the circumstances/my feelings say, *but* God's Word says … '). It is when we have given out our all, given out everything that sustains us, when the principle of death is at work in us in order that life might work in those to whom we are ministering (2 Corinthians 4:12 – following the example of the sacrificial death of Jesus which resulted in life), that we *must* learn to rise up over our feelings and tiredness and begin to confess the Word afresh in the spirit of faith, knowing that as we do, the grace that has been released to others through our lives and ministry will be imparted afresh to us by the Spirit of God in resurrection power (2 Corinthians 4:13–14 and Romans 8:11), setting us anew in a place of victory, fullness and the presence of God. Don't look to the cost, look to the reward! It is great (2 Corinthians 4:18; Hebrews 11:24–26 – this is faith that pleases God).

We can only learn to overcome and stay full of the life of God if we are a people full of His Spirit and full of His Word. We must learn to 'abide in Christ', the True Vine (John 15:1–8), if we are going to bear lasting fruit for God. In an age when the enemy has made an all-out attempt systematically to erode our convictions concerning the absolute truth and dependability of the Word of God, where in many situations *'truth lies fallen in the streets'* (Isaiah 59:14), we *must* return to the awesome power of the Word of God, trusting our very lives upon its great and solid promises. In the days that lie ahead, in fact even in the days in which we are living, there are those who have turned away from their first love (Jesus) to deceptions, some of a very supernatural nature, because they have failed to receive the love of the truth (2 Thessalonians 2:10).

Before bringing this chapter to a conclusion, let us briefly remind ourselves of the benefits of a 'Word-filled life'. The Word of God, read, meditated on (inwardly digested), believed and obeyed, gives us:

- success, freshness and consistency of life (Psalm 1:1–3);
- cleansing from and victory over sin (Psalm 119:9–11; Ephesians 5:26–27; 1 John 2:14);
- direction and guidance in life (Psalm 119:105);
- prosperity that works in any situation (Joshua 1:8);
- life and health for the physical body (Proverbs 4:20–22; Psalm 107:20);
- discernment (Hebrews 4:12);
- genuine freedom (John 8:31–32);
- restoration for the soul (Psalm 19:7);
- wisdom for life (Psalm 19:7);
- the ability to understand our true condition, thus keeping us in humility and truth (James 1:21–25);
- faith (Romans 10:17);

- impartation of the divine nature (2 Peter 1:4);
- knowledge of God's covenant promises to us (2 Corinthians 1:20);
- new birth into a living hope (1 Peter 1:23);
- assurance that every word of God is personally watched over by God Himself and He will see that it comes to pass (Jeremiah 1:12; Isaiah 55:10–11).

Knowing these truths, let us guard our hearts against the tactics the enemy uses to get the Word out of us (see Mark 4:14–20), living a life of praise no matter what the circumstances (Habakkuk 3:17–19; Psalm 34:1; Hebrews 13:15), praying in the Spirit and building ourselves up in faith (1 Corinthians 14:4; Jude 20–21). Through the Word of God and the Spirit of God, we can live lives that are literally *'strengthened with might'* (Ephesians 3:16), where we experience the reality of Paul's declaration in Philippians 4:13,

> *'I can do **all** things through Christ who strengthens me* [Greek: empowers me within].'

## Application

At the end of this chapter, rather than study questions, I would like to help you get more out of your personal times with God, by giving you three practices that have helped many a man or woman of God grow in their walk with God.

1. An old and highly respected man of God in China was once asked, 'How did you come to such a knowledge of God in your life?' His reply, 'Every day, I take a little meat and lots of potatoes!' The meat was that small portion he meditated on during the day, praying over it, confessing it and thinking over its implications and applications for his life in communion with God. The potatoes were his daily chapters that he read through on an ongoing basis, covering the Bible from cover to cover year by year, giving himself a good, solid, balanced overview of the Word of God. How can we apply this principle to our lives?

2. The Bible is made up of six natural divisions: the Old Testament historical books (Genesis – Job); the Psalms; the Wisdom books (Proverbs – Song of Solomon); the Prophets (Isaiah – Malachi); the New Testament historical books (Matthew – Acts); and the letters (Romans – Revelation). Take one book from each section, starting at the beginning (such as Genesis 1, Psalm 1, Proverbs 1, etc.), and just start reading through a chapter of each a day, or if that's too much, even a chapter a day will give you an overview of the Word every week.

3. (a) As you go through the Word, here are some questions to get you started on meditation of a given passage:
   – What does this passage tell me about the Father? The Son? The Holy Spirit? Man? Angels? The devil/ demonic?
   – Is there an example to follow?
   – Is there a command to obey?
   – Is there a promise to claim/confess?
   – Is there a sin to avoid/confess?
   – Is there a prayer to pray/item for prayer?
   Ask the Holy Spirit to speak to you and help you as you read, praying in the Spirit (tongues) before you start, opening yourself up to Him and the revelation He brings. After all, He is the Author! Be sensitive to stop and commune with the Father as you sense Him speaking to you in what you are reading. Remember this is not a race – the object is *relationship*.

   (b) Make personalised confessions of the Word from Scripture and declare them verbally every day, with thanksgiving, such as: 'Thank you, Lord, that I am a new creation in Christ, that old things are passed away, that all things are become new . . . ', etc. The Word of God is full of such truths and promises, and declaring them, standing on them with faith in your heart, releases the power of God within His Word to bring itself to pass (Romans 10:9–10).

   (c) If getting started in prayer is difficult, first ask the Holy Spirit, your prayer partner to help you. Second, many of the great 'pray-ers' of yesteryear and indeed today, use prayer-patterns, such as praying through the Lord's Prayer. Be flexible to the Holy Spirit as you do so, praying in the Spirit, worshipping the Lord and letting Him lead you – prayer was never intended to be a monologue! For example:

- *Our Father who art in heaven*: Thank Him that He is your Father, the Almighty Creator, and yet through the blood of Jesus you have become His child and can come freely into His presence – you are part of His family.
- *Hallowed be Thy name*: Begin to thank Him for who He is, declaring His promises to you in the light of His revealed character and the finished work of Calvary:
   Thank You, Lord, that You are to me:
      *Jehovah Tsidkenu*, the Lord My Righteousness
      *Jehovah Shalom*, the Lord My Peace
      *Jehovah M'Kaddesh*, the Lord My Holiness and Sanctifier
      *Jehovah Rapha*, the Lord My Healer
      *Jehovah Jireh*, the Lord My Provider
      *Jehovah Nissi*, the Lord My Banner, My Victory
      *Jehovah Rohi*, the Lord My Shepherd, Protector and Guide
      *Jehovah Shammah*, the Lord who is ever present with me!
- *Thy Kingdom come, Thy will be done*: pray for God's will to be done in national government; in Israel; in the Church; in the community; in my ministry; in my family, marriage and personal life – on earth, as it is in heaven!
- *Give us this day our daily bread*: pray for His provision and His 'now, *rhema* word'.
- *Forgive us our sins as we forgive those who sin against us*: confess sin, receive forgiveness, choose to forgive others: specifically speak it out, and set your will to forgive.
- *Lead us not into temptation*: ask Him for victory over temptation and set your will to say *'no'*.
- *But deliver us from evil*: pray a 'hedge of protection' over yourself and family etc., declare the covering of the blood of Jesus and the promises contained in Psalms 91 and 121. Through faith put on the armour of God, and receive His freedom!

- *For Thine is the Kingdom*: rejoice that His is the Kingdom, He is in control, surrender all to Him and trust Him to keep you. The government is on His shoulders.
- *Thine is the power* (yet He has given us power too!) *and the glory forever:* give it back to Him!

# Chapter 9

# The Price and Power of Forgiveness

The events of recent times, such as the tragic terrorist attacks that have been encountered around the world, are without doubt having their effect on Western society – whether it's fear, racial hatred, bitterness, anxiety, or desire for revenge. The things that we, in the West, are just starting to experience, many around the world have lived with for many years while the rest of the world has done little to help. However, for the first time, we face a serious threat to our own comfortable way of life, and a new depth of trust in God and strength of character will be needed to face and overcome the evils of our day. Anyone raised in Western democratic societies in the last thirty to forty years will be deeply conscious of their 'rights': the way in which they should be treated, the fact that their opinion matters, that they have a voice to speak and demand change. However, when expectations are not met, when we are not treated as we feel we should be, and our voice is not even acknowledged, let alone heard, we are very prone to the danger of 'taking offence'. The last four chapters of this book are not so much about external action as internal attitude, commitment and strength. One affects the other, and without both internal strength/integrity and external action, we cannot successfully overcome and victoriously finish the race God has called us to undertake (and it is the overcomers who will be rewarded, Revelation 2–3). Jesus said that it was inevitable that offences would come (Matthew 18:7), and, since that it the case, we'd better learn how to deal with them when they do, lest we be knocked out of the race (at least temporarily).

We are called to overcome evil with good, curses with blessings. We stand on the brink of perhaps the greatest challenges and opportunities for the Kingdom of God that the Western Church has faced for many years. We are called to shine the light of Jesus brightly in an increasingly dark and desperate world where the true bearers of hope will lead many to righteousness and the glory of God will be seen upon the Church in the eyes of the world. There will be cost, but great grace and great glory!

The Greek word for 'offence' is *skandalon*, from which we get the English word, 'scandal' or 'scandalous'. In ancient Greece, it was used to describe an animal trap loaded with 'bait' to attract the animal to bite and thereby be caught, snared by its lethal teeth. What an apt description! There are many believers today, even some in 'full-time' ministry, who have been snared by the power of offence. Broken promises, unjust treatment, sharp words – all provide ample opportunities to take offence, and if we succumb, we get snared! I'm sure that Joseph had many opportunities to take offence in his long journey to the fulfilment of his destiny in God! As did Jesus, betrayed by one of His own disciples, abandoned by His followers, given over to die by His fellow countrymen – and all without just reason! What's more, we are called to follow in His footsteps (1 John 2:6). We must learn the power of forgiveness, the place of dominion through blessing those who curse us, the joy of keeping our spirit free that we might continue to walk with God, bearing fruit to His glory, not 'choked' by the cares of this life (Mark 4). To die to one's own rights is to live to God! How right Corrie Ten Boom was when she said that 'to the degree that we take offence, to that degree we are still alive, we have not died to ourselves.' The way of the cross is the way of freedom, and only when we have fully embraced that cross can we truly enjoy the power of His resurrection. Consider yourself dead to offence today, and alive to God!

## What is forgiveness?

In Matthew 18:21–35 we read Jesus' parable of a servant who could not pay his master what he owed him and was thus on the verge of being stripped of all his earthly possessions and thrown into prison, together with his wife and children, until all was paid. The servant pleaded with his master, who, moved with compassion, forgave him (cancelled) all his debts! Sadly, this servant could not find it in his heart to be as forgiving to his fellow servant who owed him a much smaller sum of money, threatening him with prison if he did not pay up. Jesus said that the master's other servants, on seeing this, were so disturbed by what they witnessed that they went and told him all they had seen. This led to the master angrily throwing the wicked, unforgiving servant into prison to be tortured until he paid everything he owed. The most disturbing part of this parable comes in the last verse:

> 'So **My heavenly Father** also will do to you if each of you, from his heart, does not forgive his brother his trespasses.'
>
> (Matthew 18:35)

In this context, forgiveness is *'cancelled debt'*. It means 'I forgive you completely, no strings attached, you owe me nothing (not even an apology!).' The context of this passage is Jesus' teaching about how his disciples should deal with those who sin against them (Matthew 18:15–22). We are to initiate reconciliation, going to the brother/sister, the source of the issue, first (not talking to others about him/her – that is gossip!). If those with whom we have issue don't repent we should take someone else along as a witness. If they still don't repent, it should be told to the church, and if then there is still no repentance, Jesus said that we should treat them as if they were a heathen! Furthermore, heaven will recognise such action taken against those who refuse to be reconciled (v. 18). God places a very high premium on forgiveness.

Naturally following on from this brief discourse on reconciliation, Peter asks, *'Lord, how often shall my brother sin against me, and I forgive him? Up to seven times?'* Jesus replies, *'up to seventy times seven'* (not a literal figure, but an expression of *complete* and *endless* forgiveness). Even though it might be necessary for leaders to impose church discipline on fellow believers who refuse to be reconciled (as an act of redemptive discipline for that believer and of protection from bitterness for the church – see 1 Corinthians 5 and 2 Corinthians 2:5–11), we must keep our hearts free through forgiveness.

Such discipline may seem harsh, but it certainly underlines the fact that God, in His justice, does not tell us to do something we do not have the ability to do. He will certainly *help* us, but will not do the forgiving *for* us. That is our *choice* – feelings will follow. The Lord's Prayer and subsequent verses remind us that if we don't forgive others, God will not forgive us (Matthew 6:12, 14–15). Most of us could do with a fresh revelation of how much it cost the Lord to forgive *us*, since we are commanded to forgive *as* God in Christ has forgiven us (Colossians 3:13). We are not told to forgive to the best of our ability, or as much as we are able, but *as God in Christ has forgiven us*! That is complete. Furthermore, we are told that we should bless (*euologio*: speak well of) those who curse us, and pray for those who spitefully use us (Matthew 5:43–48). This may not be easy when you've been through great pain or abuse, but it really is both enlightened self-interest (since you get free in the process – the only one who suffers from a grudge is the person who holds it!) and Christ-like behaviour. Under the Abrahamic covenant, which is our covenant (Galatians 3:29), those who curse us get cursed, but when we bless them, we release them from receiving a curse in return – and in this way we follow the example of Jesus who died for the sins of the people who killed Him. Such blessing also brings us into a place of dominion for *'without doubt, the lesser is blessed by the greater'* (Hebrews 7:7).

Forgiveness is *not* denial. It acknowledges there is a debt, but it chooses to *cancel* it, not focus on it, to bless the offender and move on. It is a choice. Sometimes we have to make that choice many times over, particularly if we are in an ongoing situation of relational disharmony, but it is vital that we get the pain out of our hearts by consciously, verbally, and specifically forgiving those who have wounded us. That may mean speaking the forgiveness out in private as if the offender were present, specifically addressing him or her by name and saying in detail what you are forgiving him or her for. It may mean getting in touch with the person (if he or she is aware of his or her offence) or simply dealing with the issue before God (there are some things that hurt us that are solely our own issues with someone else's 'way of being/doing things', or caused by our own sense of rejection, etc. – these things we must learn to deal with before God rather than blame others). Most pain is related to events in our memories and must be disconnected from us through forgiveness (anyone, anything! Mark 11:25–26). We cannot change the past, but we can change the way we relate to it and be free from its damaging effects on our present experience. We do not have to let our past dictate our future!

## The cross – the place of exchange and basis of all forgiveness

The cross is where justice and mercy meet. It is the place where God's justice against sin (ours and others') was fully meted out so that He could freely justify those who have faith in Jesus (Romans 3:26). And herein lies the secret of forgiveness, for there is within the heart of every hurt/offended/abused person, a deep underlying sense of violation, of lack of justice. But in Christ, true justice was dispensed! The price of sin is not an apology, not a financial settlement or prison term, it is *death* (Romans 6:23; Ezekiel 18:4)! That is why God provided the blood upon the altar to make remission for our sins (Leviticus 17:11), and without that shedding of blood there can be *no forgiveness* (Hebrews 9:22). Those who sin against you are not forgiven just because you say, 'I forgive you.' They are forgiven because the price, the penalty of their sin against you, was paid in full by Jesus Christ two thousand years ago! That's why you can forgive. Without it, words of forgiveness would be empty, unjust words. But mercy can be extended because justice has been done, in Christ! Furthermore, this is the reason why the cross is the only basis of reconciliation for the world today, with all its ethnic fighting and gross injustices.

*'For He Himself is our peace, who has made both one, and has broken down the middle wall of separation, having abolished in His flesh the enmity . . . so as to create in Himself one new man*

> *from the two, thus making peace, and that He might reconcile them **both** to God in one body through the cross, thereby putting to death the enmity.'* (Ephesians 2:14–16)

When we by faith accept Christ's blood as the full price for the sins committed against us, and release mercy and forgiveness on that basis, our spirit is set free and enmity dies. Glory to God!

Then we replace unforgiveness with blessing, with prayer, with thanksgiving and praise! This keeps our spirit free. Whether or not the other person truly repents is his or her responsibility before God (Romans 12:19–21), but we must keep our hearts free.

I have been to many countries where you can almost feel the blood crying out from the ground for vengeance, in much the same ways as Abel's blood cried out to the Lord. There is an answer. The blood of Jesus speaks of better things than the blood of Abel (Hebrews 12:24)! It cries out, not for vengeance, but for mercy and, thank God, mercy always triumphs over judgement! Plead that blood for your family, your community, your nation – there is no forgiveness without it. Asking for forgiveness for the sins of your nation will achieve *nothing* without that blood, for the price of sin is *not* intercession, and *not* repentance, but death – and Jesus paid it all!

## The wisdom of God

Jesus said,

> *'Unless a grain of wheat falls into the ground and dies, it remains alone; but if it dies, it produces much grain.'* (John 12:24)

In this context, Jesus was describing His own death and the life-giving benefits that would issue forth from it. God the Father gave Jesus the Son, who died in our place, that He might receive back not only Him, resurrected and victorious, but with Him many sons to glory (Hebrews 2:10). This is the wisdom the principalities and powers did not understand (1 Corinthians 2:7–8), that out of death comes *Life*! Every time we choose to forgive, to bless, to let go of the past and let God be our vindicator, we die to ourselves and make way for the resurrection life of God to turn that impossible situation around and bring *life* out of death once more. To people who are ruled by 'sight' and natural understanding, it may look as if you are letting yourself be walked over, but before God, as you give the situation to Him, refusing to let anything be taken from you, but positively in faith sowing it as a seed to the Lord, He will turn it around, every time – for that is the wisdom of God. Paul exhorted us,

> '... *be wise in what is good, and simple concerning evil. And the God of peace will crush Satan underneath your feet shortly.*'
>
> (Romans 16:19–20)

I have personally experienced the power of this principle in my own life on a number of occasions when it seemed as if everything was being taken from me, but I went before God, refusing to fight (naturally, though I did in prayer!), and chose rather to see the situation as the greatest seed I had ever sown, since in my faith I was giving it to God, although in reality it looked as if it was being taken from me. The result? God restored everything, and more on top, more than I could have asked or thought (Ephesians 3:20). Isn't that just like our wonderful God?!

## From witchcraft to Christ

The following testimony powerfully illustrates the way forgiveness releases the dynamic grace of God into our lives.

At a Christian Summer Camp in the UK where I was ministering to the youth, before one of the sessions, in prayer I distinctly saw a vision of a young woman cutting her wrists in a satanic ritual. There was a sense in my heart that this woman would actually be in the next youth meeting and I was to minister deliverance to her. On finishing my message, I shared the vision I had received and asked if the young woman was present. Sure enough, there she was, dressed fully in black with all the usual satanic symbols hanging about her neck and body, her face looking very dark under the skin, and covered with thick black make-up, countless earrings, etc. We started to pray and very quickly she began to shake and manifest demons. However, there was no breakthrough, and I began to realise there was a deeper issue than witchcraft here. I asked her, 'Tell me, what's your real problem? This witchcraft is really just a surface issue, stemming from rebellion towards something/someone. Can you tell me what your real issue is?' The young woman suddenly became very angry in her expression, stating very strongly, 'I can never forgive him!' 'Who?' I asked. 'My father!' she snapped back. 'He abused me for years, and as soon as I could I left home. I got into heavy rock with some of my friends, then into heroine and then someone took me to the coven. I've come to this camp from there.' Satan is a legalist, and he knows that if we don't forgive, God Himself will hand us over to torment. There would be no release here until she forgave her father. I urged her, without any success, to forgive him. Finally, I asked her, 'Would you at least allow me the privilege of praying for you for grace to help you forgive? God won't do it for you, but if you are willing to receive His help, He will help you.' She agreed.

Two nights later, at the end of the evening service, I was approached by a nice-looking young lady, dressed in attractive colours, with a shining, smiling face. She said to me, 'Jonathan, I just wanted to say thank you.' I couldn't recognise her, so I asked, 'Excuse me, who are you?' She replied, 'Oh, sorry, I was the witch!' I could hardly believe it was the same girl. I asked her, 'What happened to you?' She replied, 'I forgave my father! When I did, the voices in my head instantly stopped, the drive for heroine left, and I've had no side effects!' Praise the Lord! This girl got saved, delivered from witchcraft and filled with the Holy Spirit at that camp, and all because she chose to forgive. In much the same way we have seen many people instantly healed from all manner of conditions such as asthma, heart problems, high blood pressure, arthritis, cancer, etc., financial and relational problems resolved, even new anointings and giftings released, *when they chose to forgive*. Your situation may or may not be as extreme as hers, but what God did for her, He can certainly do for you, if you will choose to walk in forgiveness.

## Forgiveness involves forgetting

God has promised, *'I will forgive their iniquity, and their sin I will remember no more'* (Jeremiah 31:34). Although there definitely is a place for speaking out one's pain to a trusted intercessor/ counsellor (and, certainly and most importantly, to God), for the purpose of getting healed and leaving the past behind, we need to recognise that we can sometimes talk something out only to talk it back in again. We have to come to the place where we close the door on the past and choose to forget. In fact, Paul urged the Philippians to do exactly that in the well-known passage in Philippians 3:13–14:

> *'... one thing I do, forgetting those things which are behind **and** reaching forward to those things which are ahead* [note the shift of focus which is vital], *I press toward the goal for the prize of the upward call of God in Christ Jesus.'*

He adds in verse 15, *'let us, as many as are **mature**, have this mind'*. Not to do so can leave us in a place where we end up nurturing bitterness and letting it take root, which Hebrews warns us, defiles many, and can even lead to other sins, in a search for false comfort, such as immorality (Hebrews 12:14–15). Forgive, close the door, and start to steer your life in a new direction by no longer talking about the past, but talking about the blessings of God and the wonderful new life you have in Him! Healing may come instantly or progressively (and it may be necessary to keep speaking forgiveness out before God until it touches your inner person and releases your emotions), but one thing is for certain, every time we speak out forgiveness, embracing the justice and mercy of the cross, we walk that much deeper in the wholeness and grace of God, live more closely to the heart of God and demonstrate more powerfully the glorious freedom of the children of God! Forgive, forget, keep a good report, and shine the light of Jesus to the world!

Let's pray:

> Father, thank You so much for the gift of Your mercy and forgiveness showered so abundantly on us through the

cross. Today I recognise that Jesus died not only for my sins, but also for the sins that have been committed against me. I make a quality decision, Lord, never to hold offence in my heart again. Help me to walk constantly in Your grace, love and forgiveness that I might help Your church to walk in unity and the power of true agreement, shining your light to the world.

[If you need to forgive anyone, do so now, as follows:] Father, I repent of holding any offence towards _____ I forgive you, _____, for _____ I release you completely from my own personal judgement, I accept the blood of Jesus as the full price for this sin against me, and I choose right now to let go of the past, forget it and move on. I bless _____ in the name of Jesus and command all bitterness or resentment to leave me now in Jesus' name. From now on I am walking in love, blessing and forgiveness. I am free. Amen.

## Application

1. Why is the cross the basis of all true forgiveness and reconciliation?

2. How easily do you take offence? If easily, why? Spend some time now asking the Lord to deal with this in your heart and help you to overcome it. (Often this can be because there are one or two issues 'way back' that we have never really dealt with, i.e. 'Father-related issues', etc. – choose to forgive today!)

3. Define 'forgiveness' as revealed in Matthew 18:21–35. How should we release forgiveness? Is forgiveness a feeling or a choice? Have you forgiven and forgotten? If not, forgive and be free today.

# Chapter 10

## Overcoming Adversity

*'My brethren, count it **all joy** [not even part of it, all of it!] when you fall into various trials [and temptations], **knowing** that the **testing** of your faith produces patience. But let patience have its perfect work, that you might be perfect [mature] and complete, **lacking nothing**.'* (James 1:2–4)

The story goes something like this: a young man walked up to Smith Wigglesworth (one of England's greatest Pentecostal evangelists of the last century) at the end of a meeting, asking him to pray that he might mature quickly in the things of God ('instant maturity' – now wouldn't that be a gift?!). Wigglesworth closed his eyes and began to pray for the young man, 'Lord, I pray that you give this man many trials and tests to his faith ...' The young man quickly stopped him, objecting strongly to the prayer. However, Wigglesworth said, 'You asked for maturity. It doesn't come any other way. To pray differently would be unscriptural!' Now that is not popular teaching. We all like the signs and wonders, the quick breakthroughs, the anointed meetings, but trials? tests? temptations? I know it's not a promise any of us claim but, nonetheless, Jesus did promise, *'In the world you **will** have tribulation; **but** be of good cheer* [count it all joy! Sound familiar?], *I have overcome the world'* (John 16:33).

We need to live in Him that we might walk in peace, having His perspective to see what is being produced, and rejoice – the breakthrough to a new level of Kingdom maturity, fruitfulness and anointing is on its way. We are living in testing times. Times of extremes, of shaking, of 'stress' (2 Timothy 3:1). We must learn to overcome by the Word of God, establishing our feet firmly in this Kingdom that cannot be shaken (Hebrews 12:28). The battle is not only external (i.e. persecutions and afflictions), but also internal (temptations). In this chapter, although I will make brief reference to the external afflictions and persecutions we sometimes face in the ministry of the gospel, the simple truth is that Satan has never really been able to hinder or stop the work of God in the church from the outside – but if the 'inside' life of a believer/leader/church can be broken or compromised, he knows that the power and life of the external ministry of the Church will cease to be such a threat to his domain. Hence, it is to this area that I will now give primary attention.

As we minister to men in our travels and ministry to churches, we often discover that the battle with issues such as pornography, whether it be on TV, the Internet or some other medium, and the immoral thoughts and deeds that flow from it, is much larger than many would like to admit, not only for our young people, but even amongst leadership. The breakdown of marriage and family life has led to divorce rates almost the same in the Church as it is in the world (and in some places equal to it!). If we truly want revival, we must face the fact that revival is for the Church. It must start with us *first*, before it will ever touch the world. The battle between 'Jezebel' (the seductive spirit that works behind pornography, immorality, relational breakdown, etc., see Revelation 2:20–23) and the end-time 'Elijah generation' is well and truly 'hotting up' (Malachi 4:5: note that the phrase 'the day of the Lord' is used in Scripture for both the first and second coming of Christ. In His first coming, John the Baptist was the 'Elijah' to come, Matthew 11:14; in His second, I believe God is raising up an end-time prophetic generation to prepare the way of the Lord, to confront nations and governments with the 'now' Word of God and the power to back it up). The facts of spiritual warfare are no excuse for bad behaviour, for it is our choices that open or close the door to the enemy – the kingdom of self and the kingdom of Satan are very closely linked! However, tolerance towards Jezebel's evil, seductive thoughts, looks and ways is something we must honestly and strongly deal with in our minds and hearts if we are going to really walk free and live with pure consciences and sincere faith. The Church *must* be able to show the world true freedom, genuine purity, and unhypocritical faith. Compromised integrity invalidates both your message and your anointing and, although it would not be profitable to present any statistics here, be assured that this is currently one of the greatest battles facing the Church's ministry, responsible for knocking more Christian leaders out of the race than one would like to recount. Problems do not disappear by ignoring them: they must be squarely faced and overcome. On the Day of Pentecost, Peter cried, *'Be saved from this perverse generation'* (Acts 2:40). Not just from hell! From sin, from a perverse age! Claiming salvation from hell without salvation from *sin* is like pronouncing a leper clean while leaving him with his disease! It's time to come afresh to the cross, embracing its work in our lives, turning from sin in genuine repentance and learning to walk in the Spirit. The aim of this chapter is to give you some keys to help you overcome and finish your race for the glory of God, not 'taken out' by the lusts of the flesh, or by the persecutions of the enemy.

Every new move of God begins with a wilderness. Moses encountered God in the desert and was sent with power to deliver the people of God. Jesus had to overcome the temptations in the wilderness before returning in the 'power of the Spirit' to Galilee. Joseph encountered great tests at every stage of his destiny in God, as the Lord refined him into the man he would need to be to save a nation in the very 'womb' of Egypt. Let's consider the steps Joseph took, the decisions he made, that took him from the life of a wandering nomad to being second only to the Pharaoh himself. (Maybe some of you reading this book will one day hold positions of great influence for the Kingdom of God in national government. Read and take note, for our decisions in private determine our success in public.)

## The power of *choice*

God has granted every human being perhaps the single most powerful right and responsibility that exists. The power of *choice*.

Choices determine our destiny, our quality of life, the impact we make for good or evil on those around us, and even affect the generations yet to come. Human beings have been given the right to choose. With that right comes authority, responsibility and consequences. What brought Joseph through the years of adversity into the high places of fulfilled destiny was his constant choice to walk in the reverential fear of God, choosing deliberately and consistently to honour Him in all his ways. And if we are faithful in the small things, God knows that we will be faithful in the large, and thus rewards us with greater and greater spheres of authority and fruitfulness in His Kingdom. In Deuteronomy 30:19 God says,

> *'I call heaven and earth as witnesses today against you, that I have set before you life and death, blessing and cursing; there-fore **choose life**, that both you **and** your descendants may live.'*

In the New Covenant the Holy Spirit has been given to us as the *parakletos*, the One who comes alongside to help. He will strengthen and empower your decision, but He will *not* make it for you! You, and only you, are responsible for the choices you make. Even in the most extreme situations, such as when Paul was in prison for his testimony of Jesus, we still have a choice. In Philippians 1:22 he expresses the fact that even though it looked as though he had no power over his own destiny (he was under Roman judgement), he still, through his own faith, had a choice. Hebrews 11 is full of testimonies of those who lived or died, *by faith*. When I was in Rwanda after the genocide, I heard accounts of those who chose to die, by faith, but confidently laid hands on others believing that they would not be harmed by anyone – and no one they prayed for was so much as even touched by the perpetrators of the crimes! We have a *choice*.

Consider these choices:

> *'... let **us** lay aside every weight and the sin which so easily ensnares us, and let **us** run with endurance the race that is set before us, looking unto Jesus, the author and finisher of our faith ...'*  (Hebrews 12:1–2)

*'I beseech you therefore, brethren, by the mercies of God, that you present your bodies a living sacrifice, holy, acceptable to God, which is your reasonable service. And do not be conformed to this world, but be transformed by the renewing of your mind, that you may prove what is that good and acceptable and perfect will of God.'* (Romans 12:1–2)

Only *you* can make those choices, but when you do, the numbers of people who can potentially be affected for the Kingdom of God can reach into the thousands. I once heard David Hogan, a brother from Mexico who has so far raised over 200 people from the dead, say, 'Obedience is my most powerful weapon!' When we are surrendered to God, in faith-filled obedience, there is nothing in heaven, earth or hell that can stop us! We are on the winning side, and *'If God is for us, who can be against us?'* (Romans 8:31). How many of us would be further on in our walk with God today had we made the right choices years ago?! How much suffering would we have saved ourselves, and others, and how much more blessing could we have brought into the world, if only we had made the right choices! We cannot go back and right those wrong choices, but we can repent, choose life today and ask God in His abundant grace to redeem those things in our lives that are the ongoing consequences of bad choices we have made in the past. He is able to do exactly that.

## Believe you have a destiny

The life story of Joseph is found in Genesis 37–48. It all began with a dream! Often when the Lord calls someone, He does so through some form of unusual supernatural manifestation, and Joseph was no exception. His dreams, while varying in content, carried the same theme. Joseph could have had a bit more wisdom in how he communicated his revelations to the family but, nonetheless, God used even his youthful ignorance and innocence to get him into position for his destiny. What followed is a heart-rending tale of hatred and betrayal by his brothers, separation from family, false accusation by his master's wife, and many long years confined and forgotten in an Egyptian prison house. But Joseph never let his dream die! The word of the Lord tested him, but it didn't let him down! Delay is *not* denial, but it is the proving of our character, the testing of our faith, and the preparation for our destiny. Never let go of your God-inspired dreams and visions! Jeremiah 29:11 says,

> ' "For I know the plans I have for you," declares the LORD, "plans to prosper you and not to harm you, plans to give you hope and a future." '
> (NIV)

> Write the vision
> And make it plain on tablets,
> That he may run who reads it ...
> Though it tarries, wait for it;
> Because it will surely come ...'
> (Habakkuk 2:2–3)

Even if the fulfilment of your vision is delayed, keep believing it, keep declaring it and praising God for it – it will not fail! In practical terms, write it down and set goals in faith, reaching out for divine strategy to co-operate with God in the fulfilling of the vision, setting in place the right structure to facilitate the work to which He has called you. And realise the vision will, like a baby being born, probably go through a period of gestation and travail before you see the final delivery! Press through in prayer and practical Spirit-led actions of faith, and the vision *will* become a reality! What we believe is so important: it determines our thinking, emotions and actions, and ultimately seals our destiny (see Numbers 13–14). If we are going to overcome adversity, we must learn to focus *not* on the impossibilities before our eyes, but on the promises God has spoken into our hearts. Remember: the things we wish God would write in the sky, He has chosen to write in our hearts through prayer (J. Cornwall)! They are no less the will of God.

God has a chosen path for each of us, a plan for every life (Ephesians 1:3–6; 2:4–10; Psalm 139:13–16). Whether or not we choose to live in that plan is *our* choice and *our* responsibility, requiring us to walk in sensitive, faith-filled relationship with the Holy Spirit who has been given to us to help us fulfil the will of God for our lives. Psalm 139 tells us that God even has a book about each one of us, where He has written every day of our lives as He wanted it to be, before we even drew breath! One day, some of us might see things in there that we've never even done! The things that God would have done through us had we obeyed, stepped out by faith and carried out the will of God. This is the difference between fatalism and predestination. You are *not* at the whim of some predetermined fate over which you have no power (as Muslims believe – 'the will of Allah'), otherwise there could be no accountability before God. The truth is, God has a predetermined plan for every one of our lives, but the choice and responsibility is ours to walk in it. In reality it is very much determined by who is really at the helm of your life – you or Him? Hopelessness and helplessness have no place in the Kingdom of God. You have a certain hope that will not disappoint (Romans 5:5) and a God who is an ever-present help in trouble (Psalm 46:1). Hopelessness is one of the chief reasons for sin's domination of so many lives (*'If the dead do not rise, "Let us eat and drink, for tomorrow we die!"'* 1 Corinthians 15:32). Without prophetic vision, people perish (Proverbs 29:18), so keep your vision alive within your heart. Stand firm and believe – He will not disappoint!

## Develop an excellent spirit

Joseph exemplified an 'excellent spirit' (heart/attitude). Perhaps his attitude could be summed up in the words of Paul to the Thessalonians,

> *'Rejoice always, pray without ceasing, in everything give thanks; for this is the will of God in Christ Jesus for you. Do not quench the Spirit. Do not despise prophecies. Test all things; hold fast what is good. Abstain from every form of evil.'*
>
> (1 Thessalonians 5:16–22)

Joseph developed patience, enduring faith, forgiveness, humility and a servant heart during his tough years of preparation (in the P.I.T. – 'Prophet In Training'). It was by no means easy – how easy it would have been to become disillusioned when the dreams/visions didn't come to pass in the expected time-frame

– but there is always special grace for tough times if we choose to receive it. When I first entered the ministry at nineteen years old, training under the ministry of another evangelist, I wanted to get straight out to win the world for Christ, but I was put to task on jobs such as envelope-stuffing, toilet cleaning, etc. I was told, 'Unless you are willing to clean the toilets, you cannot stand to minister on the platform – the greatest must be least and servant of all.' It was not what I went into the ministry for. However, I thank God for those days, which developed something in me. Relationships with others on the team weren't easy either, and all that in the midst of risking our lives to preach the gospel in dangerous locations around the world! In the midst of a number of highly pressured times I was sorely tempted just to give up and throw it all in, but I always came back to the calling. It was clear and strong within my heart: the vision had not died, and every time I turned in my heart to the Lord and recalled His words to me, declaring them with praise, there would be a fresh release of His Spirit in my heart, lifting and empowering me to keep pressing on and to walk in forgiveness, blessing and faith for the future. Paul wrote to Timothy,

> 'This charge I commit to you [a charge that he did not find easy in his natural temperament], son Timothy, **according to the prophecies** previously made concerning you, that **by them** you may wage the good warfare, having **faith** and a **good conscience** ... ' (1 Timothy 1:18–19)

Champions never give up, they get up! So move on, keep walking forward in the call of God. Your day is coming! Embrace His training, learn and develop your calling and character, taking every opportunity He gives you and doing it with an excellent heart. He always rewards the faithful!

## Choose the will of God above your flesh

We were in the Philippines, staying in a Bible college where we ministered to the students in the day and held evangelistic outreaches in the open plaza at night time, with around 500 a night coming to Christ and the Lord was confirming His word with signs and wonders. It was a great time. However, every night, when I would lay my head down to rest, my mind would start to fill with unclean thoughts that I just knew were not coming from me, and there was a very impure atmosphere around the place. The worship leader at the college, a young man, was probably one of the most anointed worship leaders I had ever met. I had seen him lead 20,000 Muslims, Catholics (of the unsaved variety), and believers into the most awesome worship where miracles of healing just started breaking out in the midst of the manifest presence of God inhabiting the praise (I am not advocating 'multi-faith' here, I am just recounting what I saw as these people were led in open worship of Jesus). The strange thing was that as I prayed about this sense of impurity, I kept thinking about this worship leader, that it was something to do with him. I wondered what to do about it, but in the end, being very busy with ministry, finally decided to do nothing except pray about it briefly, and return to the UK rejoicing in the harvest we had experienced.

My brief prayers had helped me, since I had no more battles with the unclean thoughts but, unfortunately, I had not pressed through long enough in prayer to really help the worship leader in breaking the power of that unclean spirit that was after his anointing and calling, through a weak area in his character. The following year we returned to do another mission, where this young man was again leading worship, but this time with no manifest anointing, no manifest presence of God, it was very obviously just singing and music! After the first service, I approached him to ask if he was doing OK and he burst into tears, confessing that while we were at the Bible college the year before, he was being strongly tempted to sleep with his girl-friend, but never shared this with anyone. After we left, having finished the mission, sadly, he had fallen into sin and, even though he had repented, he was still trying to regain the sensitivity and anointing he once had in his walk and ministry for the Lord. I could have kicked myself – why didn't I say something? A big lesson for me as far as the prophetic is concerned, but that is not my primary point here. This area of sexual temptation is an area that nearly every man of God I have ever met has had to face and overcome, and in many ways it is something to which we need continuously to be alert. The accounts we have in Scripture teach us the great rewards that flow towards those who overcome (such as in Joseph's case – at least after he had endured the false accusations of Potiphar's wife, and some time in prison!), and the devastating effects of yielding to its seductions, as in the accounts of Samson and David. Joseph *ran* from the scene of temptation; David was caught out by not being where he should have been (on the battlefield) and momentarily entertaining a second look; and Samson just fell headlong into fulfilling his own fleshly lusts. As with every area of life, the choice, and subsequent consequences, are ours!

## How can we protect ourselves?

### 1. Recognise that immorality is a sin against God, and against your own body

Joseph said, '*How then can I do this great wickedness, and sin* **against** *God?*' (Genesis 39:9). He recognised that, although it would be adultery and hence a sin against Potiphar and his wife, it was first and foremost a sin against God (Psalm 51:4). He chose to walk in the fear/reverence of God and thus removed himself from the place of temptation. This can be as practical for us as it was for Joseph. 'Potiphar's wife' may not be physically there (if she is, you know what to do!), but she might be on the Internet, the TV screen or in a magazine! Get up, get out, turn the TV off, get a friend to type in a secret password on your computer, restricting access if you have to, but do something! And don't allow yourself to get into a compromised position alone with your girlfriend, or spending time alone with a woman who is not your wife (even if she has come for counsel or prayer)! Think of your family, your wife and children, your reputation and how that affects others both in the church and in the world. Think about Jesus and what it cost Him to pay for your sin. Think about eternity! In 1 Corinthians 6:18 we are told that every other sin we may commit is outside the body, but sexual sin affects our very bodies, even establishing a one-flesh relationship (that should be the unique possession of our marriage partner) with someone else. The members of our bodies are literally members of Christ and we will be accountable for anything in which we involve His members (1 Corinthians 6:15). Scripture warns us strongly not to be deceived concerning these very issues. Why? Because it is quite possible to be deceived into thinking that we can live however we like, and, under grace, get away with it and still inherit the Kingdom of God. But this is *not* true (1 Corinthians 6:9–10). There is forgiveness, but we need to understand that confession of sin was provided as the emergency exit, *not* the daily staircase (Arthur Wallis)!

## 2.  Face and admit your own vulnerability, taking authority over the battlefield of the mind (2 Corinthians 10:3–4)

Every battle starts in the mind. You cannot stop the birds flying over your head, but you don't have to let them build a nest in your hair! If we entertain unclean thoughts in our minds, they will sooner or later find expression in our bodies, through such actions as masturbation or sex before/outside of marriage. The saying goes, 'Sow a thought, reap an act; sow an act, reap a habit; sow a habit, reap a destiny!' It all starts with the mind. Jesus countered Satan's temptations with the spoken word of God (Matthew 4:1–11). Jesus is the 'pattern Son', so if we follow Him, doing as He did, we will experience the victory He experienced. God's grace is not only a word of pardon if we have sinned, but a word of power to enable us not to sin. It teaches us to *say 'no!'* to ungodliness and worldly passions (Titus 2:11–12). However, if we want to be free, we must be firmly convinced in our own hearts concerning what is sin and what is not. We must be clear that 'going out with'/marrying a non-Christian is absolutely wrong (2 Corinthians 6:14) and as far as setting the context for one's future walk with God/ministry, it is sitting on a time bomb waiting to blow away your destiny!

There are other issues considered by some to be unimportant, yet in many ways weaken one's convictions and strength against more open temptation and sin. For example, there are very mixed messages in the Church concerning masturbation because it is not directly referred to in Scripture. However, whenever we face such issues of scriptural silence, we have to look to the general principles of the Word, such as:

- *'whatever is not of faith is sin'* (Romans 14:23) – can I do this in faith?

- *'let the peace of God rule* [be the umpire in your heart, deciding with all finality every issue of life] *in your hearts'* (Colossians 3:15) – does this disturb my peace?

- *'whatever you do in word or deed, do all in the name of the Lord Jesus, giving thanks to God the Father through Him'* (Colossians 3:17) – can I do this in the name of the Lord Jesus, giving thanks to God the Father through Him?

- *'He who says he abides in Him ought himself also to walk just as He walked'* (1 John 2:6) – would Jesus do this?

The body is a wonderful servant, but a terrible master! Fill your mind and heart with the Word of God to be fully persuaded and thus strengthen yourself against sin. Naturally, a married man or woman has a fully legitimate means of release as far as his or her own sexual desires are concerned, which is why Paul states the obvious in 1 Corinthians 7:8–9,

> *'I say to the unmarried ... if they cannot exercise self-control, let them marry. For it is better to marry than to burn with passion.'*

However, whatever your state, choose today and every day to be faithful to the Lord and to your marriage partner. If married give yourself fully to your partner and to the Lord. If single, give yourself fully to the Lord, releasing all your energies into serving Him and enjoying the legitimate experiences of life He has given us so freely to enjoy, and prepare yourself for the partner God has destined for you by developing the characteristics that would make you the best husband/wife anyone could wish for. Simply put, follow Jesus with all your heart, and when He brings the right one along, keep your eyes open and put some action to your faith (since *'He who finds a wife, finds a good thing, and obtains favour from the Lord'*, Proverbs 18:22)!

### 3. Ask God to change your heart, and strengthen you by His grace

Knowing that God's will is our sanctification, and that each one of us must learn *how* to possess his or her own body in self-control (read 1 Thessalonians 4:3–8 – it is strong stuff), we should ask God to change and purify our hearts, and strengthen us by grace, praying, 'Lord, lead me *not* into temptation, and deliver me from evil.' The moment you think you are invulnerable to sin, you are entering a dangerous place of deception and vulnerability. We are new creations in Christ, but the vital, experiential part of that is that we are to *'put off ... the old man ... and be renewed in the spirit of your minds and ... put on the new man which was created according to God, in true righteousness and holiness'* (Ephesians 4:22–24). Grace is available for everyone who asks for it – so ask, and you *will* receive! God is constantly trying to bring us to a place of total dependence on Him – that is where struggles cease and victory is realised: when we enter into the rest of faith, believing in our deliverance in Christ (Colossians 1:13–14).

### 4. Understand the nature of temptation

Temptation is *not* sin, otherwise Jesus sinned (which we know He did not). Don't allow the enemy to bring you under condemnation, but do recognise the warning bells! In 1 Corinthians 7:5 and James 1:14 Scripture clearly indicates that we are much more prone to the devil's temptations when either we have failed to deal with ungodly desires *in ourselves*, or we are lacking in *self-control*. Proverbs tells us that a person without self-control is like a city without walls – anything can get in! Therefore we must allow God to put His finger, by His Spirit and His Word, and the godly admonition of fellow believers, on the areas of our lives that need change, and learn to walk in the Spirit. Spend time redeeming those old desires and thought patterns by truth-replacement therapy, i.e. put the Word of God and the presence of God in their place – reverse it to disperse it! The simple fact is that everyone faces temptation (1 Corinthians 10:13) and God will not allow you to be tempted beyond what you can bear! He will show you the way out, if you will ask Him and take it!

Furthermore, when you do overcome, you'll enter a whole new plane of victorious Kingdom living and dominion (James 1:12). Welcome to the zone of accelerated growth!

### 5. Make yourself accountable
Thank God for the Body of Christ!

> 'Confess your trespasses to one another, and pray for one another, that you may be healed.' (James 5:16)

I used to think this verse was just for Catholics! I thought that, as a believer, I only needed to confess my sins to Jesus, my Great High Priest, and I would be forgiven (1 John 1:9; 2:1). Well, that's true, *but!* It also became quite a convenient way of side-stepping any accountability to the Body of Christ, of which I am a part, and which my sin affects and, let's face it, some of us are just too ashamed, fearful, or proud to confess our sins to another brother or sister in Christ! We can spend so much time trying to project and live up to a 'victorious 24–hours-a-day' image that we actually cut ourselves off from the Body and place ourselves in a position of great vulnerability. I am not saying that we should go around confessing every little failure to anyone we can find who will listen but, if we are struggling in an area of our lives, we need to have the openness, honesty and vulnerability to ask for help without fearing that somehow we are going to be 'written off' and our 'dirty washing' hung up for everyone in the Body of Christ to see. We must learn to trust, and to be trustworthy in the things that others share with us/confess to us. As my father says, we need to learn to be a 'full-stop' in the Body of Christ. The ability to love enough to cover and restore our struggling brothers and sisters in the Church is much needed in the day in which we are living. Such accountability provides a forum for a person to receive cleansing, healing and deliverance, if necessary (it is possible for believers to 'give place to the devil' through sin, and get themselves bound), and to be built up again to a place of fruitfulness and ministry. Furthermore, the need for leaders to be accountable, to have genuine, trustworthy friendships where they can relax, open up and share their hurts, needs, temptations, etc., is vital. I am personally convinced that many of the recent moral failures amongst leadership in the Body of Christ would never have happened had the Church not put her leaders up on such a platform, where they operate more like the managers of a large corporation or business, and no one can get close enough to them to help them and stand with them in their humanity. We are all brothers and sisters first – leadership and anointings must always come second!

In closing this paragraph, just a quick cautionary note. Accountability can never be forced: it can only be offered by the one desiring to make him or herself accountable. Be very cautious about accountability to someone who is not prepared to open up his or her life to you also. Furthermore, since such vulnerability does lead to true heartfelt fellowship (*koinonia*: literally, 'sharing', 'close association', 'opening the door of your heart to let someone else in'), do not under any circumstances start such accountability with a member of the opposite sex who is not your marriage partner. Frankly, having such an open-hearted accountability should be part of your ongoing communication with your spouse anyway.

### 6. Walk in the Spirit

Galatians 5:16 urges us, *'Walk in the Spirit, and you shall not fulfil the lust of the flesh.'* Ultimately, to live in victory, we must learn a new walk, a new lifestyle of vital relationship with the Holy Spirit. To do so is to walk free from the flesh, and from the law. There is a very real danger, when one considers the issues we have looked at in this chapter, in swinging right over from licence to legalism, which in the final analysis will only put you under law and take you back into sin. The real key is relationship. Therein is found the centre road, the way of liberty, the highway of holiness. It is unachievable without Christ. We have been made righteous by the gift of God's grace and, as we walk in fellowship with Him, we are ever being transformed more and more into His likeness. If you have fallen already and failed in the area of immorality, just confess your sin to God, repent and go on with Jesus. Make yourself accountable to a Christian leader you can trust, who can help you re-establish yourself in your walk with God. Remember, even if you have to take some time out of ministry to go through a process of restoration, 'time out' does not mean 'out for good'! To fail does not make you a failure! There is full restoration in Jesus – your Redeemer lives. There is a wonderful passage in the Gospels in which Jesus said, *'the altar sanctifies the gift'* (Matthew 23:19). Place your body afresh on the altar of personal commitment to Christ, offering it to Him as a living sacrifice, and be sanctified, cleansed and free. Change your focus and start to walk in the Spirit, daily spending time in His presence in prayer and the Word of God, living in fellowship with Jesus and your brothers and sisters in Christ. Always remember: relationship before function!

In closing this chapter, it is worth stating again that Joseph walked in the fear and honour of God, He never let go of his dreams and vision through bitterness or unforgiveness, impurity and even unbelief. He recognised that the rejection of his brothers actually turned out for their good, and the good of many others. It was, as someone once said, 'a life-saving rejection'. If we will recognise the hand of God in our situations, staying prayerful in the Holy Spirit (Romans 8:26–28 – this is not automatic, you need to be praying in the Spirit), keeping a good and faithful heart, we will see not only the life-changing, character-transforming grace of God making us into the vessels of His choosing, but the redeeming power of God step in at the perfect time to release us from every adversity and catapult us forward into the destiny of God for our lives. And believe me, when God's 'suddenly' comes, things turn around very quickly indeed! Keep praising Him, for the battle is the Lord's and His Word will *not* return void!

Let's pray:

> Heavenly Father, I thank You today for Your life-changing grace at work in me. I offer my body to You as a living sacrifice, holy and acceptable in every way. Lord, please help me to walk in purity of heart and life, living consistently before You. I want to honour Your name in all my thoughts, words and deeds. Cleanse me from sin and strengthen me to walk in grace, love and forgiveness, believing You are in control and will bring to pass Your purpose in my life. I

choose to be an overcomer today. I will not focus my eyes on the past but on the great future You have for me in Christ. Thank You that the work You have begun in me You will bring to completion.

In Jesus' name. Amen.

## Application

1. What power/responsibility has God granted to every human being, and what are its consequences (Deuteronomy 30:19)?

2. Consider Ephesians 2:4–10 and Psalm 139:13–16. In what ways have you seen God's sovereign hand directing the course of your life and ministry thus far? Take courage and thank Him – He who has been faithful thus far will be faithful to complete the work He has begun in you (Philippians 1:6)!

3. What prophetic vision has God given you for your life/ministry? Take some time to write it down and consider prayerfully what steps you could take to see the vision come to pass. Remember, God works through human vessels – we are 'co-workers with Him' in His great plan!

4. Review the section 'How can we protect ourselves'? What action do you need to take to ensure that you are able to overcome temptation and thus fulfil your destiny in Christ?

# Chapter 11

# The Meek Shall Inherit the Earth

'Meekness' and 'militancy': they don't really seem to mix, do they?! Jesus came to *'destroy the works of the devil'* (1 John 3:8), yet He was described as *'the Lamb of God'* (John 1:29), and young children loved to climb up into His lap and be blessed by Him – something that Jesus clearly delighted in (Luke 18:16). He was not afraid to denounce fiercely the religious leaders of the day, drive out the sellers in the temple with a whip, and even describe Herod, a truly violent political leader, as a 'fox', yet He was deeply moved with compassion by the needs of the people (Matthew 9:36), lamented for those who rejected Him (Matthew 23:37), and prayed for forgiveness for those who crucified Him (Luke 23:34). No wonder Paul pleaded with the Corinthians by *'the **meekness** and gentleness of Christ'* (2 Corinthians 10:1). Meekness, far from being the 'weak' and 'fragile' quality the world would label it, is actually a characteristic of the mighty and the blessed, for Jesus, the King of kings and Lord of lords, is described as 'meek' (Matthew 11:29), and it is the 'meek' who shall *'inherit the earth'* (Matthew 5:5). Moses, described as *'very humble, more than all men who were on the face of the earth'* (Numbers 12:3 – obviously, until Christ), had such a ministry under God that the 'epitaph' given him by the Scriptures is that,

> *'... since then there has not arisen in Israel a prophet like Moses, whom the Lord knew face to face, in all the signs and wonders which the Lord sent him to do in the land of Egypt before Pharoah, before all his servants, and in all his land, and by all*

*that mighty power and all the great terror which Moses performed in the sight of all Israel.'*     (Deuteronomy 34:10–12)

The days are coming, indeed they are already upon us, when God is calling 'Moses ministries' to confront the evil Pharaohs of our day, with their openly wicked and unrighteous governments. The cost ahead for some of us might be great, but the great 'I AM' is with us, just as He was with Moses. The grace and the reward will be greater than the cost. Let us be those whom God can trust with His power, the 'meek' who shall inherit the earth.

In writing a book with a title such as *Militant Christianity*, I am well aware that some might read it and go away with an attitude like James and John who wanted to call down fire from heaven to burn up a village of Samaritans when they wouldn't receive Jesus (Luke 9:51–56). Jesus rebuked them (interestingly enough, the Greek text uses the same word as when Jesus 'rebuked' a demon), telling them that they did not know what *spirit* they were of and that He had not come to destroy people's lives but to *save* them. We must be 'militant' towards Satan and his evil cause, but 'meek' towards God, and 'meek' towards our fellow human beings. As the Body of Christ arises in these last days, to confront the enemy's advance in our nations, boldly proclaiming the Kingdom of God, we must be ready to correct,

> **'in humility** . . . *those who are in opposition, if God perhaps will grant them repentance, so that they may know the truth, and that they may come to their senses, and escape the snare of the devil* . . . '     (2 Timothy 2:25–26)

Let's consider this wonderful Christ-like quality, and the great promises of God that accompany it.

## Meekness – what is it?

Vine's *An Expository Dictionary of New Testament Words* says, 'the meekness manifested by the Lord and commended to the believer is the fruit of power. The common assumption is that when a man is meek it is because he cannot help himself; but the Lord was meek because He had the infinite resources of God at

His command. Described negatively, meekness is the opposite to self-assertiveness and self-interest: it is equanimity [evenness of mind or temper – Chambers] of spirit that is neither elated nor cast down, simply because it is not occupied with self at all.'

Meekness is grace under pressure, strength under control, having the characteristics of gentleness and humility. It is often associated with wisdom and the fear of God. In James 1:21, we are instructed to receive the Word with all meekness. It has the quality of teachability, in stark contrast to the pride and independent attitudes of many a Western culture today. In 1 Thessalonians 1:2–10 and 2:13, one cannot help but make the connection between the way the Thessalonians received the Word of God from the apostles (as the Word of God, not the words of men), and the way in which the gospel came to them in power and much assurance. The benefit we derive from the Word of God depends almost entirely on the way in which we receive it. The values of the Kingdom of God are diametrically opposed to the values of this world system. The Lord declared, *'My grace* [charis] *is sufficient for you, for my power* [dunamis: miracle-working ability] *is made perfect in weakness* [Greek: inability to produce results]' (2 Corinthians 12:9 NIV). Paul, in response, declared, *'Therefore I will boast all the more gladly about my weaknesses, **so that Christ's power may rest on me.'** Oh how we need to hear this! I remember a time when I was conducting a mission in East Anglia, England. We had seen many people come to Christ that week, and quite a number of healings, deliverances, etc., but by the last night, at the end of a busy mission and a busy summer, I was exhausted and ready to go home. At that very moment, as we were closing the mission, a whole line of people who had not responded to 'words of knowledge' and prophetic words during the week, suddenly decided that 'now' was the time to come forward for prayer! I can honestly say that normally I am very gracious with people who respond for prayer, but at this point I was feeling considerably 'stretched'. I began to pray for the first person, sensing no anointing at all, and faith was certainly *only* expressed in action since all I could feel at that moment was a sort of exhausted 'numbness'. However, before I could even lay hands on the first person, they fell under the power of God and were instantly healed. I was amazed – what had I done? Nothing! What did He do? Everything!

Every person I went to pray for that night had the same experience, and they were all suffering from major conditions: cancer, arthritis, deafness – no headaches and stomach problems here! As I went along the line of people praying, I couldn't help but sense the Lord's pleasure in demonstrating His power through my obvious weakness at that moment. The simple truth is that if we really want to move with God, allowing Him to do what He wants to do through us, it is not so much a case of 'trying' as it is of 'yielding', 'trusting'. The power of God is like supernatural electricity – the less the resistance, the greater the flow of power. In the words of Paul, *'when I am weak,* **then** *I am strong'* (2 Corinthians 12:10).

## Powerful promises for 'meek' believers!

1.  God's provision and real satisfaction:

    *'The* **meek** *shall eat and be satisfied.'*                    (Psalm 22:26)

2.  Guidance:

    *'The meek He guides in justice,*
    *And the meek He teaches His way.'*                    (Psalm 25:9)

    Let's face it, it's hard to learn anything when you think you know it all already. If you walk in 'meekness' you'll have the best teacher there is!

3.  Inheritance:

    *'... the meek ... shall inherit the earth.'*        (Matthew 5:5)

    The first Adam was God's 'under-ruler' but lost everything through sin. The issue in Adam partaking of the tree of the knowledge of good and evil was not primarily over mere knowledge – that he could have through relationship with the Father. The real issue was the source of the knowledge – himself (reason) or God (revelation). In essence, it comes down to: independence or dependence, pride or humility. Pride is a mark of Satan's rule; humility is a mark of God's. Interestingly, however 'strong' the proud may appear, humility is always greater and always outlasts and overcomes pride – just look at the cross! The mighty but meek Saviour overcame death and ransomed the world back to God through the way of meekness!

4.   Salvation and deliverance:

> *'God arose to judgement,*
> *To deliver all the meek of the earth.'*                    (Psalm 76:9)

> *'He will beautify the meek with salvation.'*               (Psalm 149:4)

5.   God's exultation over the enemy:

> *'The Lord lifts up the meek,*
> *He casts the wicked down to the ground.'*                  (Psalm 147:6)

6.   Increased *joy*:

> *'The meek also shall increase their **joy** in the Lord.'*
>                                                            (Isaiah 29:19)

7.   Victorious spiritual warfare:

> *' "God resists the proud,*
> *But gives grace to the humble."*
> **Therefore**, *submit to God. Resist the devil and he will **flee** from you . . . Humble yourselves in the sight of the Lord, and He will lift you up.*                    (James 4:6–10)

8.   A carefree life:

> *' . . . all of you be submissive to one another, and be clothed with humility, for "God resists the proud, but gives grace to the humble." Therefore, humble yourselves under the mighty hand of God* [clearly a place of power since "the hand of God" was symbolic for the power of the Holy Spirit in the Old Testament in miracles, judgement, discipline and blessing], *that He may exalt you in due time, casting all your care upon Him, for He cares for you.'*          (1 Peter 5:5–7)

9.   A quality that beautifies (makes attractive):

> *' . . . the incorruptible beauty of a gentle* [meek], *and quiet spirit, which is very precious in the sight of God.'*
>                                                            (1 Peter 3:4)

Meekness is something that is seen as being very beautiful, and very precious in the eyes of God, particularly with reference to the character of a woman.

## 'Reckless meekness'

If we really want to make an impact on this generation (which is everything contrary to what we have just described – see 2 Timothy 3:1–5 for a very 'apt' description of our present generation), we are going to have to demonstrate a different spirit entirely. Right from the beginning of our new life with Jesus we learn that humility is a mark of His reign in our lives, indeed fundamental to Kingdom living. Jesus said, 'unless you humble yourselves as little children and be converted, you will by no means enter the Kingdom of God' (see Matthew 18:3). While it is true that we should grow up in the Kingdom, we must never lose the intrinsically childlike qualities of simple faith, humility and the desire to learn and conquer new abilities and tasks. Without those fundamental qualities, we will cease to walk in any dimension of power or revelation whatsoever, and fail hopelessly to demonstrate to the world the great joy of a simple, trusting relationship with Jesus. We would find ourselves moving from the heartfelt reality of a new love and life with Him to the dead, predictable and desperately 'safe' arena of the mind, bound up with religious formalism and theological argument. God can do so much more with the slightly reckless and dangerously trusting attitude of a young child than He can with the 'mature' 'balanced' approach of the person who has done it all, seen it all, grown a little cynical and too safe for their own good (is this really 'maturity'?), despite their degree in theology and many years' experience in ministry! I am all for taking a responsible approach to leadership, but not at the expense of seeing the power and life of the Kingdom of God break out through Holy-Spirit-led reckless faith that changes the community. Is this part of 'meekness'? Certainly! Toward God! And the fruit that flows from it, expressed in lives radically changed by the grace and power of God, is a wonder beyond words. Meekness does certainly *not* mean 'weakness', compromising the Word of God or the leading of the Spirit of God for the sake of pleasing men – Jesus, the Word made flesh, meekness personified, *never* did that.

## Jesus – the pattern of meekness

Jesus exhibited an attitude of total surrender to the Father's will. His loathing for the religious system of the day that kept people bound in legalism and bereft of the true knowledge of God sometimes brought out the 'lion' part of His nature, but even then His words, though strong, were measured by the Spirit of God within Him, for He only said what He heard the Father say (John 14:10). The Holy Spirit like a dove could descend *and remain* on Him who had the Lamb nature (John 1:29–34). Isaiah prophesied that the Spirit of God would *rest* on Him (Isaiah 11:2), even though He is the Spirit of counsel and *might*. Philippians 2:5–11 tells us how Jesus humbled Himself as a man, taking the very form of a servant, dying on a cross for you and me, in perfect submission to the Father. The result: He was exalted to the *highest* place, and given the name at which every knee will bow and every tongue confess that *Jesus Christ is Lord*. Through the cross, the ultimate demonstration of meekness, Jesus stripped Satan of his armour and authority, redeemed mankind and inaugurated His new creation which will one day culminate in a new heaven and a new earth in which right-eousness dwells and His saints will reign forever with Him. The meek *shall* inherit the earth!

## Meekness: the saving of a nation

Meekness is part of the fruit of the Holy Spirit, sometimes translated as 'gentleness' in our modern English Bibles. It is developed through a sincere, heartfelt walk with God in the life and power of the Holy Spirit. It's possible for each one of us to live in such a way because the Spirit of God has been given to us to enable us to walk as He walked. However, such a walk is not only attractive, it is imperative! Nations are changed one life at a time! If we want revival we can have it, but it must start with *us*.

It means humbling ourselves before God, being willing to submit ourselves to Him, His Word, His Way of doing things, dying to our own opinions and concerns of what others may think or do to us and living wholly for Christ. God *'sought for a man'* (Ezekiel 22:30), and He still does! Not only an individual, but a corporate man, the Body of Christ. The time to awaken to righteousness, to humble ourselves, to reach out in faith-filled intercession and bold, uncompromising proclamation of the gospel is *now*! The time to demonstrate His love to the broken and needy (Matthew 25:31–46) and release His power through faith and compassion to the sick and dying is *now*! The time to speak up for righteousness and truth in our nation is *now*! God's time is *now* (2 Corinthians 6:2)! Immediately before His ascension, Jesus commanded the disciples to wait in Jerusalem until they received the promise of the Father. The disciples were still so desperate to know if Jesus would at last restore the Kingdom to Israel. They still had their *own* agenda, their *own* dreams and visions, but Jesus said,

> *'It is **not** for you to know times or seasons which the Father has put in His own authority. **But** you shall receive power when the Holy Spirit has come upon you; and you shall be witnesses to Me* [literally: My martyrs] *in Jerusalem, and in all Judea and Samaria, and to the end of the earth.'*          (Acts 1:7–8)

Times and seasons are God's business to reveal as and when He chooses, but world evangelism is our commission and our responsibility. God has given us His Word, His authority and His power to back it up. The time is *now*. Will you arise, lay down your own agenda, your own dreams, and live for *his*? Generations to come lie in the balance!

William Booth, the founder of the Salvation Army, declared, 'The chief danger of the twentieth century will be: religion without the Holy Ghost, Christianity without Christ, forgiveness without repentance, salvation without regeneration, Heaven without Hell.' Thank God for the great moves of God that were experienced in the twentieth century ensuring that some of the dangers Booth prophesied did not come to full reality, by the mercy of God! But the dangers he prophesied are perhaps even more valid at this juncture in history when, as we stand at the beginning of a new millennium, the needs are even greater, the challenge even deeper, and a new generation is arising who have not known the ways and power of God as former generations have known Him. God is able *and* willing, but are we? If history teaches us anything, it teaches us that when people respond to the prophetic word in faith, when people get desperate and thirsty enough for God that they will seek Him, cry out to Him and do *whatever is necessary* for His Kingdom to come in power and glory and reverse the tide of evil in the nations, *God answers.* It is high time for this generation to arise out of its comfort zone and give sacrificially, live dangerously (i.e. whatever the cost) and stand uncompromisingly for the Kingdom of God. The old saying has stood the test of time and proven true again and again, 'All it takes for evil to prevail is for good men to do nothing!' Passivity in time of crisis is a great and far reaching evil. Knowing what is good, but not doing it is sin. If we truly believe that God hears our prayers for revival, we must act in faith, going out to proclaim with words, works and wonders the good news of the Kingdom, expecting results. Faith without action is dead, but faith expressed in action releases the power and glory of God!

Let's believe His promise,

> *'if My people, who are called by My name will* **humble themselves***, and pray and seek My face, and turn from their wicked ways,* **then** *I will hear from heaven, and will forgive their sin and heal their land.'*　　(2 Chronicles 7:14)

Let's obey His word,

> **'Go** *into all the world and preach the gospel to* **every** *creature.'*　　(Mark 16:15)

Let's expect His promise,

> *'And this gospel of the kingdom* **will** *be preached in all the world as a witness to all the nations, and then the end* **will** *come.'*　　(Matthew 24:14)

> *'but truly as I live, all the earth* **shall** *be filled with the glory of the* Lord.*'*　　(Numbers 14:21)

Amen! Come, Lord Jesus!

Let's pray:

> Father, I humble myself under Your mighty hand. I surrender all that I am and all that I have to You and the call You have placed upon my life. Make me and mold me into the vessel You have created me to be. I yield fully to Your purpose and plan for the glory of Your name and the extension of Your Kingdom. Help me to walk in true Christlike meekness, walking in love, grace and humility towards all people, yet never compromising Your truth nor obedience to Your ways. Change, challenge and strengthen me until my love be shown in true service, my commitment in selfless sacrifice, my faith in works of power and my devotion in unfeigned worship and glory to You. As I stand before You, Lord, I believe and confess that You can and will change my generation. I know You are looking for willing and available vessels through which to display the glories of Your love and power. I hear Your call saying, *'Whom shall I send? And who will go for us?'* Lord, here am I, send me. Thrust me forth into the harvest fields, equipped with your grace, Your anointing and Your love. May I be found faithful, truly fruitful, giving You the glory that is Yours and Yours alone.
>
> In Jesus' name, Amen.

### Application

1. In what ways did Jesus combine meekness and militancy? How can we?

2. In what ways do you need to embrace the meekness of Christ in your own life and ministry?

3. What is your response to Jesus' commission to *'**Go** into all the world and preach the gospel to **every** creature'* (Mark 16:15)?